Ebaholz Campus-Erweiterung
Campus Extension

Bauprozess im Entwurfsstudio
Building as a Common Process

Carmen Rist-Stadelmann
Urs Meister
(Hg. / eds.)

Universität Liechtenstein
University of Liechtenstein

PARK BOOKS

Ort des Austauschs 7
Place of Exchange 9

Holzverbindungen —
Ein realisierbarer Anspruch? 18
Wood Joints —
A Feasible Aspiration? 19

Das Ebaholz-Projekt und
der menschliche Massstab 35
The Ebaholz Project
and Human Scale 37

Die Weichheit des Holzes 40
The Softness of Wood 41

Prozess oder Produkt 57
Process or Product 59

Inhalt Contents

Prototypen
Treppe und Wand 69 / 91
Prototypes
Staircase and Wall 69 / 91

Farbe und Raum 81
Colour and Space 83

Raum im Raum 103
Space Within Space 105

Erfahrungen als
Bauherrenvertreter 120
Experiences as
Client Representative 121

Factbox 137
Fact Box 139

Quellenangabe List of References 141
Impressum Imprint 142

Ort des Austauschs
Place of Exchange

Carmen Rist-Stadelmann
Urs Meister

„Der Raum ist ein Geflecht von beweglichen Elementen.
Er ist gewissermassen von der Gesamtheit der Bewegungen erfüllt,
die sich in ihm entfalten. […] Insgesamt *ist der Raum ein Ort,
mit dem man etwas macht.*"

Michel de Certeau[1]

Das Zusammenspiel von Räumen zum Arbeiten, Lernen und Lehren veränderte sich in den letzten Jahren merklich. Zwanzig Jahre nach dem Bezug des denkmalgeschützten Fabrikbaus der ehemaligen Spoerry-Spinnerei in Vaduz hatte sich die Universität Liechtenstein in diverse Aussenstellen in umliegenden Wohnhäusern und einem weiter entfernten Bürobau ausgebreitet und verfügte nicht mehr über zeitgemässe räumliche Identität. Mit der Übernahme einer Liegenschaft, die in der Nähe des Campus neu erstellt wurde, sollte der Zersplitterung der Arbeitsorte begegnet und eine Konzentration auf zwei klare Standorte erreicht werden. Die neuen Flächen, die sich in einer wesentlich exponierteren Lage an der Hauptstrasse befinden, erforderten eine massgeschneiderte Intervention mit räumlichen und gestalterischen Antworten auf die Fragen, welche das Räderwerk der Zusammenarbeit innerhalb der Universität Tag für Tag neu aufwirft.

Das Advanced Studio Craft & Structure von Urs Meister und Carmen Rist-Stadelmann der Liechtenstein School of Architecture bekam die einzigartige Möglichkeit, die Campus-Erweiterung zu entwerfen. Der

Innenausbau wurde von den Architekturstudierenden im Austausch mit Experten aus Szenografie, Akustik, Holzbau und Farbgestaltung entwickelt und in Kooperation mit regionalen Handwerksbetrieben ausgeführt.

In einem wechselseitigen Prozess wurde die Schaffung von Möglichkeiten für soziale Interaktion innerhalb der Grenzen des neuen Rohbaus ausgelotet. Das Studio experimentierte mit Holz, Textilien und Farben, befasste sich mit den verschiedenen Aspekten, die Raum und Atmosphäre für kreative Teamarbeit bieten, und folgte der Idee des One-to-One mit dem Bau von Prototypen in einer Werkhalle und direkt auf der Baustelle.

Der Neubau im Ebaholz beherbergt heute neben Räumen für die Weiterbildung und die Business Law School gemeinsam genutzte Seminarräume, eine Aula sowie einen Teil der Verwaltung der Universität. Die Kombination von Unterrichtsräumen und Einzelbüros neben flexiblen Lern- und Arbeitslandschaften stellt als Resultat einer gelungenen Kooperation von unterschiedlichsten Akteuren ein multifunktionales Werkzeug für die Universität dar.

'Thus space is composed of intersections of mobile elements. It is in a sense actuated by the ensemble of movements deployed within it. […] In short, *space is a practiced place*.'

Michel de Certeau[1]

The synergy of spaces for working, learning and teaching has changed markedly in recent years. Twenty years after moving into the listed factory building of the former Spoerry spinning mill in Vaduz, the University of Liechtenstein had expanded into various satellite locations in neighbouring residential buildings and a more distant office building, and thus no longer had a contemporary spatial identity. By taking over a newly built property close to the campus, the intention was to counteract the fragmentation of workplaces and achieve a concentration in two distinct locations. The new spaces, located much more prominently on the main road, required a tailor-made intervention with spatial and design responses to the questions that are raised anew day after day by the machinery of collaboration within the university.

The Liechtenstein School of Architecture's Advanced Studio Craft & Structure, led by Urs Meister and Carmen Rist-Stadelmann, was given the unique opportunity to design the campus extension. The interior fit-out

was developed by the architecture students in collaboration with experts in scenography, acoustics, wood construction and colour design, and then carried out in cooperation with regional skilled-trade contractors.

A back-and-forth process was used to explore the creation of opportunities for social interaction within the confines of the new building shell. The studio experimented with wood, textiles and colours, examined the various aspects that provide space and atmosphere for creative teamwork, and followed the idea of working at 1:1 scale by building prototypes in a workshop and directly on the construction site.

The new building in Ebaholz now accommodates not only rooms for continuing education and the Business Law School, but also shared seminar rooms, an auditorium and part of the university administration. The mix of classrooms and individual offices in combination with flexible learning and working landscapes is the result of a successful collaboration among a wide range of actors and represents a multifunctional tool for the University.

Entwicklung und Präsentation Development and presentation

Entwicklung und Präsentation Development and presentation

Entwicklung und Präsentation Development and presentation

Holzverbindungen — Ein realisierbarer Anspruch?
Wood Joints — A Feasible Aspiration?

Klaus Zwerger

Die Universität Liechtenstein baute sich eine kleine, treppenförmige Aula. Bei der sehr schlichten Holzkonstruktion springen die Verbindungsdetails ins Auge. Wenn wir von Holzverbindungen hören oder sprechen, denken wir heutzutage – beeinflusst von Gebrauchsobjekten, die uns umgeben –, zumeist an Fingerzinken oder Schwalbenschwänze. Es gab Zeiten, als Schreiner Verbindungen entwickelten, die für den Betrachter und die Betrachterin eines Möbels nicht sichtbar waren. Das Bestreben, die Verbindung verdeckt zu gestalten, konnte ein Konstruktionsdetail mitunter erheblich verkomplizieren. In Japan schufen die Zimmerleute – die in der Regel auch den Innenausbau innehatten –, im Grossen gesehen generell „unsichtbare" Verbindungen, im Innen- wie im Aussenbereich. Die klimatischen Bedingungen erzwangen eine solche Entwicklung für den Aussenbereich. In jeder Verbindung tritt Hirnholz zutage. Das ist aber der verletzlichste Teil eines Holzstücks gegenüber Bewitterung. Aus dieser Not entsprang die Tugend, Hirnholz als unschön zu klassifizieren und so weit als möglich aus dem Blickfeld zu verbannen.

Ich wage zu behaupten, dass heute mehr denn je die Durchschnittsnutzenden eines Möbels kein wirkliches Interesse daran haben, wie es zusammengebaut ist. Diverseste Verdübelungstechniken haben den Zusammenbau von Elementen beschleunigt, für die Konsumierenden verbilligt und die jahrelange Praxis von Handwerkern obsolet werden lassen. Wenn heute Verbindungen sichtbar ausgeführt werden, steht eine andere Idee dahinter. Diese Details sollen eine Botschaft von solider traditioneller Holzarbeit vermitteln. Liebhaber und Liebhaberinnen lassen sich dann Möbel produzieren, in die verschiedene Holzarten eingefügt werden oder kunstvoll eingesetzte Verbinder aus einer anderen Holzart zum Einsatz gelangen. Wichtig ist ihre Sichtbarkeit. Sie sollen Aufmerksamkeit auf sich ziehen.

Ich darf den erwähnten Einbau der Aula an der Universität Liechtenstein zum Anlass nehmen, über den Begriff Holzverbindung nachzudenken.

Was ist die Aufgabe von Holzverbindungen?

Sie sollen Kräfte möglichst verlustfrei von einem Holzelement zum anderen übertragen. Das gelingt heute theoretisch besser als früher. Gepresste Holzfasern, verleimte Holzstücke und andere Holzwerkstoffe sind vieler ihrer dem Ursprungsmaterial inhärenten Eigenschaften beraubt. Wenn der gewachsene Zellverbund aufgelöst ist, verlieren Phänomene wie schwinden, verdrehen, reissen ihren Schrecken. Proportional zum Zerspanungsgrad reduziert sich die Mühe, das Material genau zu untersuchen, um es optimal einzusetzen. Eine gezielte Wahl des besten Materials war immer eine ökonomische Frage. Kaiser Yongle liess für die Bereitstellung des Holzes Nanmu für die von ihm 1421 eingeweihte Verbotene Stadt in den damals kaum erreichbaren Provinzen Yunnan und Sichuan die Wälder plündern und das geschlägerte Material nach Beijing transportieren. Die letzten reinen Holzklaviere wurden aus Fichten produziert, die es noch in den Urwäldern Rumäniens gab. Diese Ressourcen sind erschöpft. Wir wollen jedoch die Diskussion über noch vorhandene Urwälder aussparen. Gepflanzte Wälder und Plantagenbäume decken den immens gestiegenen Bedarf. Ihre Verarbeitung zu denaturierten Holzprodukten kompensiert ihre mindere Qualität. Sie erlaubt insbesondere einen weitgehenden Verzicht auf dereinst unumgängliches Wissen um die Materialeigenschaften.

The University of Liechtenstein has built a small, integrated stepped seating element for their aula. The joint details of this very simple wooden construction are quite striking. Today, influenced by the everyday objects that surround us, when we hear or talk about wood joints, we usually think of finger joints or dovetails. There was a time when carpenters developed furniture joints that were invisible to the beholder. Trying to conceal the connection could sometimes complicate a design detail considerably. In Japan, the carpenters—who were responsible not only for exterior work but usually for interior work as well—generally created 'invisible' joints, both inside and out. The climatic conditions made this a necessity for the exterior areas. Every joint has some exposed end grain. But this part of any piece of wood is the most vulnerable to weathering. So it needs the most protection. This necessity has led to the end grain being considered unattractive and therefore hidden as much as possible.

I dare say that today, more than ever, the average user of a piece of furniture has no real interest in how it is put together. A wide variety of dowelling techniques have speeded up the assembly of elements, made the results cheaper for the consumer and made long-standing practices of craftspeople obsolete. Today, when joints are made to be seen, there is a different idea behind the decision. Such details are intended to convey a message of solid, traditional woodwork. Connoisseurs can have furniture made in which different types of wood are joined together, or in which connectors of a different type of wood are artfully inserted. The important thing is that they are visible. They are meant to attract attention.

I would like to take the aforementioned construction of the stepped aula seating at the University of Liechtenstein as an opportunity to reflect on the notion of a wood joint.

What is the purpose of a wood joint?

A wood joint should transfer forces from one wooden element to another with as little loss as possible. In theory, this is better achieved today than in the past. Pressed wood fibres, glued wood pieces and other engineered wood composites are divested of many of the inherent properties of the original material. When the natural cell structure is broken down, phenomena such as shrinkage, warping and cracking become less of a concern. The effort required to analyse the material in detail in order to utilise it optimally decreases in proportion to the degree to which it is machined. Choosing the best material has always been a matter of economics. To obtain nanmu hardwood for the Forbidden City he inaugurated in 1421, the Yongle Emperor ordered the forests in the then almost inaccessible provinces of Yunnan and Sichuan to be plundered and the timber transported to Beijing. The last pianos made entirely of wood were made from spruce trees that were still found in the virgin forests of Romania. These resources are now exhausted. But this is not the place to discuss the remaining virgin forests. Planted forests and plantation trees meet the huge increase in demand. Processing them into denatured wood products compensates for their inferior quality. In particular, it has made it possible to largely dispense with the once indispensable knowledge of material properties. Although plantation trees are still individuals, they are sufficiently uniform and easy to handle to be machined without difficulty.

Machined joints are absolutely precise. This type of production, which is intended to

Plantagenbäume sind zwar immer noch Individuen, aber ausreichend gleichförmig und bearbeitungsfreundlich gezogen, um sie problemlos maschinell verarbeiten zu können.

Maschinell hergestellte Verbindungen sind absolut passgenau. Diese Fertigung, die ökonomische Vorteile bringen soll, muss in puncto Spezialisierung und Individualisierung Abstriche machen. Viele handwerklich entwickelte Verbindungen sind somit von einer Übersetzung in maschinelle Herstellung ausgeschlossen. Das ist per se kein Problem, weil viele Verbindungen aus handwerklichem Ehrgeiz und nicht aus konstruktiven Überlegungen entstanden.

Gilt die geforderte verlustfreie Kräfteübertragung für alle Holzverbindungen?

Holzverbindungen werden dann zur Denksportaufgabe, wenn sie die Bewegungsmöglichkeit zweier oder mehrerer Holzelemente einschränken bzw. lenken, aber nicht gänzlich unterbinden sollen. Denken wir an Blockbaufügungen, an Rahmen- und Füllungskonstruktionen, wie sie in der Architektur Stabkirchen und viele Speicher prägen, oder an die Gratleiste in Flächenverbindungen.

Eine Sonderform der Blockbaufügung ist in den ostasiatischen Kragkonstruktionen verwirklicht. Kragarme werden mit grossen und kleinen Holzblöcken zusammengesteckt mit dem Ziel, horizontale Last möglichst weit über vertikale Lastträger oder schützende Wände auskragen zu lassen [Abb. 1]. Je weiter ein Dach über eine vertikale Holzkonstruktion auskragt, desto besser ist die Konstruktion geschützt. Diese Konsolen dienen nicht nur der Erweiterung der Traufe. Sie werden auch — wir sollten sagen, vor allem — zum Aufbau der Dachkonstruktion [Abb. 2] und in gewissem Ausmass zur Verbindung der das Dach tragenden Säulen eingesetzt. Am leichtesten erkennbar ist ihre Funktion der Lastbalance. Die Auskragung nach einer Seite wird durch eine Auskragung nach der anderen Seite ausgeglichen [Abb. 3].

Kopfbänder erzielen diese Wirkung in der okzidentalen Architektur. Einem vertikalen Element wird ein horizontales Element aufgelegt und muss naheliegenderweise gegen ein Kippen nach der einen oder anderen Seite gesichert werden [Abb. 4]. Das Kopfband verbindet die beiden Elemente zu einem winkelstabilen Dreieck, das einen solchen Kippeffekt verhindert. Wenn der Lasteintrag zu massiv ausfällt, wird das Dreieck zerstört und die Balance der Konstruktion aus dem Gleichgewicht gebracht [Abb. 5]. Der Kollaps, die totale Zerstörung, kann die Folge sein. In der orientalischen Bautradition wird ein vergleichbarer Effekt durch sukzessives weiteres Auskragen von übereinander gelegten Kragarmen erzielt. Die Übereinanderschichtung der einzelnen Elemente mit reversiblen Verbindungen verleiht ihnen die Chance, auch auf heftige Lasteinträge flexibel zu reagieren. Flexibel insofern, als die einwirkenden Kräfte auf Elemente treffen, die nicht unnachgiebig fixiert sind. Zugleich — und erst das lässt das Konzept wirklich aufgehen —, besteht eine solche Kragkonsole aus vielen Elementen, nicht drei unverschiebbar fixierten. Die grosse Anzahl der Elemente erlaubt die Verteilung des Lastangriffs auf viele Elemente. Die Belastung von wenigen Verbindungen wird auf viele verteilt. Die Grenzen der materialimmanenten Elastizität können nicht verschoben werden. Aber je weniger das einzelne Element eines Knotens belastet wird, desto widerstandsfähiger kann ihre Summe reagieren und desto eher kann die Konstruktion ins Gleichgewicht „zurückpendeln". Die „weiche" Fügung verhindert, dass Verbindungen zerstört werden.

Holzverbindungen — Ein realisierbarer Anspruch?

1 Shanxi, Wutai, Doucun, Foguang si (857), China. Foguang Temple (Foguang si, 857), Doucun, Wutai County, Shanxi Province, China.

2 Shanxi, Yangqu, Fanzhuang, Dawang miao (1467), China. Dawang Temple (Dawang miao, 1467), Fanzhuang, Yu County, Shanxi Province, China.

3 Zhejiang, Ningbo, Hongtang, Baoguo si (1013), China. Baoguo Temple (Baoguo si ,1013), Hongtang, Ningbo, Zhejiang Province, China.

bring economic benefits, has to make compromises in terms of specialisation and customisation. As a result, many joints developed by skilled woodworkers cannot be translated for machine production. This is not a problem in itself, as many joints are the result of artisanal ambitions rather than constructional considerations.

Do all wood joints have to transmit forces without loss?

Designing wood joints becomes a challenging mental exercise when they are intended to restrict or guide, but not completely prevent, the movement of two or more pieces of wood. Think of the interlocking joinery used in log construction, frame and infill construction, such as that used in the architecture of stave churches and many storehouses, or the dovetail batten used to join boards together to form a surface.

A special form of interlocking joinery is used in East Asian cantilevered structures. Cantilevers are created by interlocking large and small timber blocks to allow horizontal loads to project as far as possible over vertical load-bearing posts or protective walls [fig. 1]. The more a roof cantilevers beyond a vertical timber structure, the better the structure is protected. These brackets are not only used to extend the eaves. They are also, and in fact primarily, used to build up the roof structure [fig. 2] and to a certain extent to connect the columns that support the roof. Their load-balancing function is the most easily recognizable. The cantilever on one side is balanced by a cantilever on the other side [fig. 3].

In occidental architecture, this is achieved by using angle braces. A horizontal element is placed on top of a vertical element and must,

Wood Joints — A Feasible Aspiration?

Statische Überlegungen sind ein Aspekt, optische ein anderer. Wenige kuppel- und tonnenförmige Konstruktionen in Skelettbauweise kommen in der okzidentalen Architektur ohne Zugbänder aus [Abb. 6]. Kopfbänder schaffen einerseits erst den Eindruck der Wölbung, beeinträchtigen ihn aber gleichzeitig [Abb. 7]. Nach innen verschalte Konstruktionen verschleiern dies nur. In der orientalischen Bauweise illusionieren Kragkonstruktionen – wie sie im Westen etwa in Steinbauten eingesetzt wurden –, die Kuppel deutlich glaubhafter [Abb. 8].

Können wir schliessen, dass eine nachgiebige Verbindung besser ist als eine absolut fixe?

Mit dieser Frage tun sich viele weitere auf. Ist „nachgiebig" gleichzusetzen mit „nicht passgenau"? Gibt es überhaupt fixe Verbindungen? Wann sind Verbindungen perfekt? Eine analytische Auseinandersetzung mit diesem Fragenfeld führt zum Ergebnis, dass die Frage nicht sinnvoll ist. Sie lässt viele Überlegungen ausser Acht, ohne die die Beschäftigung mit ihr unseriös bleibt. Je nach Verbindung ergeben sich andere Aufgabenstellungen.

Ein aufschlussreiches Beispiel für notwendig andere Denkansätze in historischer und zeitgenössischer Herstellung ist die Gratleiste. Ein keilförmiges Brett in einem Bretterboden, in den wandbildenden Stäben der Stabkirchen oder in Wänden und Böden von Getreidespeichern reagiert auf sich ändernde Luftfeuchtigkeit. In kleinerem Massstab, also aus näherer Distanz sichtbar, soll die Gratleiste in Kleinarchitekturen wie Möbeln denselben Effekt erzielen. Flächig nebeneinander gelegte Bretter sollen durch eine orthogonal eingegratete Leiste an ihrem Ausweichen aus der ebenen Fläche gehindert werden. Zugleich muss die Leiste das

4 Markthalle in Beaumont-de-Lomagne (14. Jh.), Tarn-et-Garonne, Occitanie, Frankreich. Market hall in Beaumont-de-Lomagne (14th century), Tarn-et-Garonne department in Occitania, France.

5 Zehntscheune Great Coxwell Barn (13. Jh.), Faringdon, Oxfordshire, England. Great Coxwell Barn tithe barn (13th century), Faringdon, Oxfordshire, England.

6 Taubenhaus der Ferme de Vaulerent, Villeron, Val-d'Oise, Frankreich. Dovecote of the Domaine de Vaulerent, Villeron, Val-d'Oise department in Île-de-France, France.

Holzverbindungen – Ein realisierbarer Anspruch?

7 Dormitorium der Abbaye de Fontenay (Dachkonstruktion 15. Jh.), Bourgogne, Frankreich. Dormitory of the Abbey of Fontenay; roof construction, 15th century), Marmagne, Côte-d'Or department in Bourgogne-Franche-Comté, France.

8 Dieses im Rahmen einer Ausstellung an der China Academy of Art in Hangzhou präsentierte Anschauungsmodell entstand unter massgeblicher aktiver Mitarbeit von Prof. Liu Yan an der Kunming Universität. Illustrative model presented as part of an exhibition at the China Academy of Art in Hangzhou, created with the crucial active collaboration of Professor Liu Yan of Kunming University of Science and Technology.

of course, be secured against tilting to either side [fig. 4]. The angle brace joins the two elements to form a fixed-angle triangle that prevents such overturning. If too much load is applied, the triangle will be overstressed and destroyed, upsetting the balance of the structure [fig. 5]. Collapse and total ruin can be the result. In the oriental building tradition, a comparable effect is achieved by successive further projections of superimposed cantilevers. By stacking individual elements and connecting them reversibly, they can respond flexibly to heavy loads. Flexibly in the sense that the forces acting on them are resisted by elements that are not rigidly fixed. At the same time — and this is what makes the concept really work — such a cantilever bracket consists of many elements, not three fixed elements. The large number of elements allows the application of load to be distributed over many elements. The load of a few connections is distributed over many. The limits of the material's inherent elasticity cannot be shifted. But the less the individual element of a node is stressed, the more resistant their sum can react, and the faster the structure can 'swing back' into equilibrium. The 'soft' assembly prevents the joints from being destroyed.

Structural considerations are one aspect, visual considerations are another. In Western architecture, very few dome- and barrel-shaped skeletal structures do without tie bars [fig. 6]. On the one hand, angle braces give the impression of vaulting, but at the same time they detract from it [fig. 7]. Constructions that are clad on the inside only disguise this. In Asian construction methods, cantilevered structures — such as those used in stone buildings in the West — give a much more credible impression of the dome [fig. 8].

Quellen und Schwinden der Bretter quer zu ihrer Faserrichtung, also ihre Bewegung erlauben. Wie das Beispiel der multifunktionalen Treppenskulptur in Liechtenstein zeigt [Abb. 9], kann diese Verbindung sehr schnell und höchst präzise mit einem Fräser hergestellt werden. Der Reibungswiderstand beim Einschlagen der Gratleiste wächst mit der Anzahl der zu verbindenden Bretter. Der Bewitterung im Aussenraum preisgegeben, kann eine Gratleiste mit parallelen Gratkanten schnell zu einer sichtbaren Einschränkung ihrer zugedachten Aufgabenbewältigung führen. Ein durch Verwinden festgeklemmtes Brett kann das Gleiten der benachbarten Bretter verhindern.

Die Herstellung der Gratleiste mit Gratsäge, ausstemmen und Grundhobel war aufwendig und niemals „perfekt". Die Zimmerleute halfen sich mit einer konischen Gratleiste. Der Reibungswiderstand beim Fügen liess sich auch durch eine mehrfach abgesetzte Gratleiste verringern. Sie war aber nicht vergleichbar festgefügt. Die manuell hergestellte Gratleiste war trotz ihres Herstellungsaufwands eine sehr häufige Verbindung. Sie konnte leicht nachgeschlagen werden und Einzelteile liessen sich leicht auswechseln.

Der Gedankengang der konischen Fügung machte insbesondere im skandinavischen Blockbau [Abb. 10] die Kombination mit Skelettbauweise möglich. In Japan legten die Zimmerleute ihre langen Zapfen mit Auszugswiderstand, wie beispielsweise den Sichelzapfen, konisch an, um ihn nicht schon bei der Fügung zu beschädigen. Der gleichen Idee folgten chinesische Zimmerleute bei zahlreichen Details komplexer Knoten [Abb. 11]. Apropos Blockbau: Tür- und Fensterrahmen mussten mit verdeckten Zapfen eingebaut werden. Der jeweilige Zapfenkopf musste deutlich kürzer als das Zapfenloch im Balken

Holzverbindungen—Ein realisierbarer Anspruch?

9   Detail der Treppenskulptur, Aula Universität Liechtenstein.
Detail of the stair sculpture in the aula of the University of Liechtenstein.

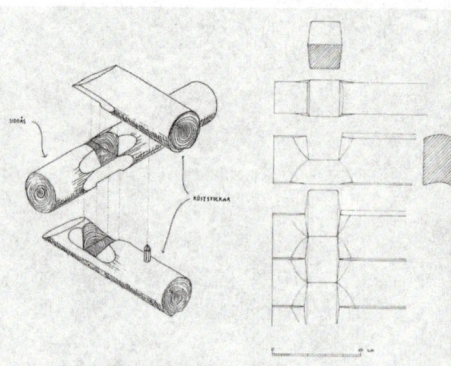

10   Detail eines norwegischen Blockbaus (aus: Peter Sjömar; „Byggnadsteknik och timmermanskonst"; Abb. 98). Detail einer finnischen Blockbaukirche (aus: Lars Petterson; „Templum Saloense" Helsinki, 1987: Abb. 273). Detail of Norwegian log construction (source: Peter Sjömar, 'Byggnadsteknik och timmermanskonst' [Building techniques and the art of the carpenter], doctoral dissertation, Chalmers University of Technology, extract from fig. 98). Detail of a Finnish block-pillar church (source: Lars Petterson, *Templum Saloense*, Helsinki: Suomen Muinaismuistoyhdistys, 1987, fig. 273).

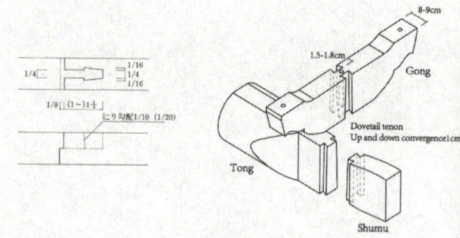

11   Die Schultern des Sichelzapfens sind nicht vertikal, sondern leicht winkelig geschnitten. Der männliche Teil gleitet (ohne Reibungswiderstand) von oben in den weiblichen Teil (aus: Uchida Yoshichika; „Zairai kōhō no kenkyū" Tokyo, 1993: Abb. 4-2-2). Detail einer „gestapelten Eimer-Konstruktion" (stacked bucket structure) als Ergebnis ihrer intensiven Feldforschung zur *shumu*-Konstruktion in Fujian und Guangdong, von Meng Yang gezeichnet. The shoulders of the gooseneck tenon are not cut vertically, but at a slight angle. The male part slides into the female part from above (without frictional resistance) (source: Uchida Yoshichika, *Zairai kōhō no kenkyū*, Tokyo, 1993, fig. 4-2-2). Detail of a 'stacked bucket structure' drawn by Meng Yang as a result of her intensive field research on *shumu* construction in Fujian and Guangdong provinces.

Can we conclude that a flexible connection is better than an absolutely rigid one?

This question raises many more. Is 'yielding' synonymous with 'not precisely fitting'? Are there any rigid joints at all? What makes a perfect joint? An analytical examination of this range of questions leads to the conclusion that the question is not a meaningful one. It ignores many considerations without which it remains of questionable value. The requirements vary according to the type of joint.

A revealing example of the need for different approaches in historic and contemporary production is the dovetail batten. A wedge-shaped board in a plank floor, in the wall-forming staves of a stave church, or in the walls and floors of a granary responds to changes in humidity. On a smaller scale, that is, visible at close range, the dovetail batten is intended to achieve the same effect in small-scale architecture such as furniture. Boards laid side by side in a plane are prevented from deviating from that flat plane by a batten orthogonally dove-tailed into the surface. At the same time, the batten must allow the boards to swell and shrink perpendicular to the grain—in other words, it must allow them to move. As the example of the multifunctional stair sculpture in Liechtenstein [fig. 9] shows, this joint can be produced very quickly and with great precision using a milling cutter. The frictional resistance when hammering in a dovetail batten increases with the number of boards being joined. When exposed to outdoor weathering, the intended performance of a dovetail batten with parallel grooves can quickly become visibly impaired. A board that has become wedged tight by warping can prevent the adjacent boards from sliding freely.

Making the dovetail using a dovetail saw, chisel and router plane was labour intensive and never 'perfect'. To help, carpenters used a batten with tapered sides. The frictional resistance of the joint could also be reduced by using a stepped dovetail. In comparison, however, it was not as firmly joined. The handmade dovetail remained a very common joint, despite the effort involved in making it. It was easy to tighten with a hammer blow and the individual parts were easy to replace.

The idea of conically tapered joints made their use possible in combination with skeletal construction, particularly in Scandinavian log construction [fig. 10]. In Japan, carpenters tapered their long, pull-out-resistant tenons, such as the gooseneck tenon, so that they would not be damaged during the joining process. Chinese carpenters followed the same idea for numerous details of complex nodes [fig. 11]. Apropos log construction: door frames and window frames had to be installed with concealed tenons. The head of each tenon had to be considerably shorter than the mortise in the beam, so that the vertical framing element did not restrict the movement of the beams in between. The tenons were concealed to keep the construction 'clean'. Is such a joint no longer a perfect fit? Is it still friction-locked?

Do the workpiece, the tool and the craftsperson have a relevant influence?

When carpenters pre-dried dowels, the idea was to allow the dowel to swell in the dowel hole. But this was nothing other than deliberately dimensioning them so they would *not fit*. This idea often went hand in hand with the use of different types of wood. Hardwood has short fibres, whereas softwood has long fibres.

sein, damit das vertikale Rahmenholz die Bewegungsfähigkeit der Balken dazwischen nicht einschränkt. Die Zapfen wurden verdeckt ausgeführt, damit die Konstruktion „sauber" blieb. Ist eine solche Verbindung nicht mehr passgenau? Ist sie noch kraftschlüssig?

Ist der Einfluss von Werkstück, Werkzeug und Handwerker von Relevanz?

Wenn Zimmerleute Dübel vortrockneten, war die Idee dahinter, die Dübel im Dübelloch aufquellen zu lassen. Das heisst aber nichts anderes, als sie wissentlich „unpassend" zu dimensionieren. Oftmals war diese Idee mit der Verwendung verschiedener Holzarten verknüpft. Laubholz hat kurze Holzfasern, Nadelholz lange. Die Zimmerleute passten ihre Verbindungsdesigns diesen Materialeigenschaften an.

12 Jedes Vollholz reisst, durchaus in Abhängigkeit von Qualität und Trocknungsprozess. Die herumgewickelten Bambusstreifen sollen Abhilfe schaffen, können es aber nur kurzfristig. All solid wood will split, depending on the quality and drying process. The bamboo strips wrapped around the timber are intended to provide relief but can only do so for a short period of time.

    Wenn ein gewohntes Material nicht mehr zur Verfügung stand, musste auf eine andere Holzart zurückgegriffen oder nicht zufriedenstellende Materialqualität akzeptiert werden. Das kann schnell zur Akzeptanz wenig konstruktiver Hilfsmassnahmen führen, die die Lebensdauer des Objekts nicht massgeblich verlängern [Abb. 12]. Die chinesischen Zimmerleute arbeiteten in diesem Fall nicht grundsätzlich weniger exakt [Abb. 13] als im Vergleichsbeispiel Jodo-ji in Japan [Abb. 14]. Die Beispiele springen in ihrer Gegensätzlichkeit ins Auge. Sie verstellen damit allzu leicht eine von vielen Überlegungen, die in ihrer Gesamtheit über die Werthaltigkeit einer Verbindung entscheiden. Wir sehen sofort, dass im einen Fall die Materialqualität fragwürdig ist. Zumindest dürfen wir sagen, dass das Material fragwürdig eingesetzt ist. Im anderen Fall können wir nur annehmen, dass die Säulen anlässlich der letzten Rekonstruktion 1632 überlegt

13 Die übereinander geschnittenen Zapfenlöcher begünstigen die Ausbildung des Risses entlang der vertikalen Achse dieser Löcher. Die Kragarme können dem auflastenden Gewicht nachgeben, weil das Zapfenloch um den Riss verbreitert ist. Der schräge Kragarm wirkt als Hebel zur fortgesetzten Verbreiterung des Risses. The series of mortises cut on top of each other facilitated the formation of the crack along the vertical axis of these holes. The cantilevers are able to yield to the imposed load because the mortise is widened around the crack. The tilted cantilever acts as a lever to further expand the crack.

14 Jōdo-ji jododo (1194), Hyōgo. Das Detail einer der vier Innensäulen zeigt, wie stark eine Säule perforiert werden kann, ohne Schaden zu nehmen. Jōdo Hall (Jōdo-ji jododo , 1194), Ono, Hyōgo Prefecture, Japan. This detail of one of the four inner columns demonstrates how much a column can be perforated without being damaged.

Carpenters had adapted their joint designs to these material properties.

If a familiar material was no longer available, a different type of wood had to be used, or a material of unsatisfactory quality had to be accepted. This can quickly lead to the acceptance of less structural remedial measures that do not essentially extend the service life of the object [fig. 12]. In one such case, the Chinese carpenters worked with no less precision [fig. 13] than in the comparative example of Jodo-ji in Japan [fig. 14]. The examples are striking in their contrasting nature. They all too easily obscure one of the many considerations that, taken as a whole, determine the intrinsic value of a joint. We can immediately see that in one example the quality of the material is questionable. At the very least, we can say that the material has been used in a dubious way. In the other example, we can only assume that the columns were judiciously chosen for the last reconstruction in 1632. What we may not be paying enough attention to is the fact that in one example the columns are outside and in the other they are inside.

Stone tools cannot produce the same results as those made of iron. Steel is not typically Damascus steel. Fascinating results have been achieved by artisans throughout the ages. To speak of better or worse seems dubious. Technologies have always been developed in response to the possibilities available. Good tools need to be treated with respect. The best Japanese tools are only as good as they can be if they are sharpened perfectly every day.

A beginner needs better tools than an expert. But only an experienced master can get the best out of a tool. Either way, it is up to the craftsperson to handle materials and tools well or badly. The lack of perfectly suitable raw

Wood Joints — A Feasible Aspiration?

ausgesucht wurden. Worauf wir vielleicht nicht ausreichend achten: Die einen Säulen stehen aussen, die anderen innen.

Steinwerkzeug kann nicht gleiche Resultate liefern wie solches aus Eisen. Stahl ist nicht Damaszenerstahl. Faszinierende Ergebnisse schufen Handwerker aller Zeiten. Von besser oder schlechter zu sprechen, erscheint unseriös. Technologien wurden immer als Antwort auf zur Verfügung stehende Möglichkeiten entwickelt. Gutes Werkzeug verlangt respektvolle Behandlung. Die besten japanischen Werkzeuge sind nur so gut, wie sie täglich perfekt geschärft werden.

Ein Anfänger braucht besseres Werkzeug als der Routinier. Aber nur der routinierte Meister kann aus einem Werkzeug herausholen, was in ihm steckt. So oder so liegt es am Handwerker, gut oder schlecht mit Material und Werkzeug umzugehen. Der Mangel an idealem Rohstoff oder an optimalem Werkzeug zwingt den Handwerker zu Flexibilität in der Nutzung des Angebots. Erst die Akzeptanz mangelnder Verfügbarkeit und weniger optimaler Ressourcen mündet in der Änderung gewohnter Techniken, schafft Innovation.

Eine handwerklich ausgeführte Verbindung kann nicht perfekt sein. Dennoch hängt von ihrer Ausführung (und mehr oder weniger einfachen Auswechselbarkeit!) die Lebensdauer des Objekts ab. Eine aus zwanzig, dreissig oder mehr Teilen bestehende ostasiatische Kragkonsole muss zwangsläufig Ungenauigkeiten aufsummieren. Wir dürfen davon ausgehen, dass die Zimmerleute um dieses Defizit Bescheid wussten. Warum hielten sie dennoch daran fest? Wir können diese Frage nicht beantworten. Wir müssen aber konstatieren, dass sich ein erfahrener Handwerker sehr wohl den Kopf zerbricht, ob er eine tradierte Konstruktion oder ein gesehenes Konstruktionsdetail ändern muss, weil es Schwächen aufweist. Wir wissen aus Erfahrung, dass Defizite im Bauen in aller Regel nicht mit der Reparatur eines Details in Ordnung gebracht werden können. Sie müssen Anlass sein, die Schritte neu zu überlegen, die in dem problematischen Detail münden. Der verantwortungsbewusste Handwerker muss also weit mehr Faktoren berücksichtigen als die perfekte Passgenauigkeit eines Details.

Greifen wir die Eingangsfrage noch einmal auf, ob der Anspruch, den der einzelne mit dem Begriff Holzverbindung in Zusammenhang bringt, erfüllbar ist. Ehrlicherweise müssen wir darauf ausweichend antworten. Es hängt von der Erwartungshaltung ab. Was soll die Holzverbindung leisten? Die Geschichte zeigt, dass Handwerker unvorstellbar komplizierte Verbindungen entwickelten, die sogar singuläre Erscheinungen bleiben konnten. Niemand wollte sie nachbauen, weil sie dem Auftraggeber in ihrer Ausführung zu kostspielig waren und ihr Nutzen in keiner Relation zum Aufwand stand. Umgekehrt gibt es gar nicht wenige Beispiele, in denen Auftraggeber willens waren, mehr, vielleicht sogar viel mehr zu bezahlen, um auf diese Art Distinktionsmerkmale zum Nachbarn zu schaffen. Der Zimmermann konnte glücklich damit sein, wenn er freie Hand erhielt, um zu zeigen, wozu er imstande war. Der Handwerker konnte aber auch daran Gefallen finden, etwas geschaffen zu haben, das als Rätsel bestehen blieb. Holzkonstruktionen sind vergänglich. Wenn sie sich überleben, gehen mit ihnen alle Details unter. Vielleicht stellt sich der eine oder die andere die Frage nach dem unsichtbaren Innenleben und muss akzeptieren, dass er die Antwort niemals erhält. Das kann die heimliche Freude des Herstellers bleiben.

materials or optimal tools forces the craftsperson to be flexible in the use of what is available. It takes the acceptance of insufficient availability and suboptimal resources to change familiar techniques and create innovation.

A handcrafted joint cannot be perfect. Nevertheless, the longevity of an object depends on its design (and on the ease with which it can be replaced!). An East Asian cantilever bracket consisting of 20, 30 or more pieces is bound to have inaccuracies. We can safely assume that the carpenters were aware of this shortcoming. So why did they hold on to it? We cannot answer that question. What we can say, however, is that an experienced woodworker will certainly give a great deal of thought to whether a traditional construction or a particular design detail needs to be changed because it has weaknesses. We know from experience that construction flaws cannot usually be remedied by repairing a detail. They must be a reason to rethink the steps that led to the problematic detail. A responsible craftsperson must therefore consider many more factors than just the perfect fit of a detail.

Let us return to the question we started with: Is it possible to fulfil the aspirations that people associate with the idea of wood joints? To be honest, we have to give an evasive answer. It depends on the expectations. What is the wood joint supposed to do? History shows that woodworkers have developed joints of unimaginable complexity that have actually remained singular phenomena to this day. No one wanted to reproduce them because they were too expensive for the client and their benefits bore no relation to the effort involved. Conversely, there are more than a few examples of clients willing to pay more, perhaps much more, to create features that set them apart from their neighbours. The carpenter could be happy to be given a free hand to show what he or she could do. But the artisans could also to take pleasure in having created something that remained a mystery. Wood constructions are ephemeral. When they become obsolete, all the details disappear with them. Perhaps someone or other has asked themselves the question about the invisible inner workings and had to accept that they never received an answer. This can remain the secret joy of the maker.

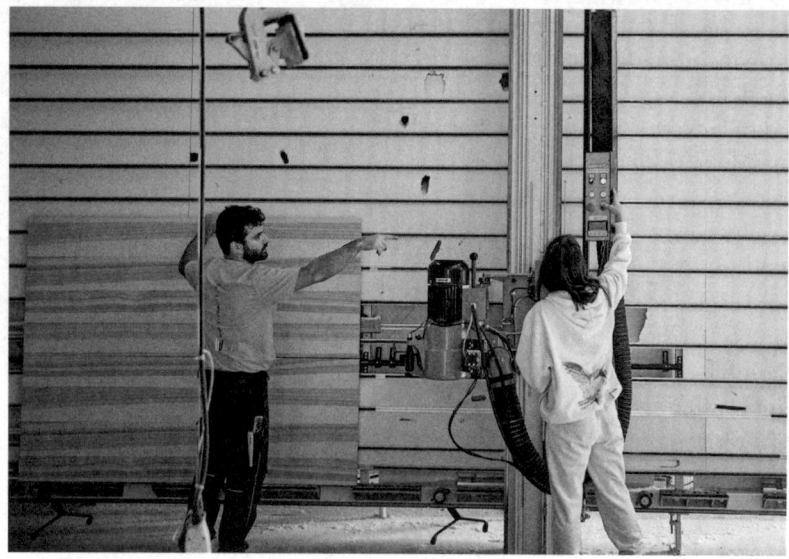

Produktion Production

Produktion Production

Das Ebaholz-Projekt und der menschliche Massstab
The Ebaholz Project and Human Scale

Machiel Spaan

An der Kreuzung Landstrasse und Fürst-Franz-Josef-Strasse in Vaduz steht ein scheinbar anonymes Bürogebäude aus Beton und Glas. Ein klares, graues Fassadenraster verrät die Grösse und den Massstab des „Bürohauses". Zwischen zwei Pfeilern befinden sich jeweils ein Doppelfenster mit Brüstung oder ein Einzelfenster mit einer grauen Fläche daneben. Die vorgefertigten Fassadenelemente sind abstrakt detailliert. Sie zeigen wenig Handschrift des Erbauers. Obwohl gut proportioniert, wirkt das Gebäude wie eine Dutzendware, es fehlt eine Seele. Im Gegensatz zu dieser anonymen Fassade haben Studierende der Universität Liechtenstein im Herzen des Gebäudes eine Intervention vorgenommen, die dem Gebäude auf mehreren Ebenen einen menschlichen Massstab verleiht.

Haus im Haus

Das von den Studierenden gebaute Holzvolumen mit einer Grundfläche von fünf mal fünf Metern und einer Höhe von vier Metern bildet ein bescheidenes und markantes Volumen in der Mitte des Bürogebäudes. Das Volumen enthält eine Küche, einen Lagerraum und Kommoden. Das Volumen gewährt Raum für Begegnungen, Bewegung und Präsentation. Das hölzerne Objekt bietet den Besuchenden des Raumes Orientierung. Es ist ein Angelpunkt im Zentrum des Gebäudes. Die Treppe und die Tribüne verbinden räumlich und physisch das erste und zweite Stockwerk des Büros.

Das Volumen schafft einen intimen Raum, der mich einerseits an Albrecht Dürers Tafelbild „Der heilige Hieronymus im Studierzimmer" erinnert [Abb. 1], ein hölzernes Volumen als Arbeitsraum in der Mitte des grossen Raumes. Andererseits aber auch an das faltbare Haus, das der Künstler und Filmemacher Jeroen Kooijmans zusammen mit Studierenden der Akademie für Architektur gebaut hat [Abb. 2]. Ein flexibler Ort für Begegnungen und Gespräche, der die Umgebung offen miteinbezieht.

Das Objekt besetzt das Herz des Gebäudes mit einem Treffpunkt zum Sitzen, Zeitverbringen, Stehen und Bewegen. Stufen, um die Treppe zu erklimmen, Flächen zum Sitzen, Kanten zum Abstützen, ein Lattenrost zum Anlehnen. Es definiert den Innenraum. Bietet einen warmen und menschlichen Massstab.

Mehrdeutiger Raum

Die Treppe und die Podeste sind mehr als nur eine vertikale Verbindung. Das Volumen beherbergt mehrere praktische Funktionen wie die Küchenarbeitsfläche unten, die halbhohen Regale im oberen Geschoss und den Stauraum und die Schubladenauszüge unter der Tribüne. Vor allem aber schafft das Objekt einen Ort des Aufenthalts und der Begegnung. Ein Aufenthaltsort, der nicht klar definiert ist und mehrfach genutzt wird: vom Gesprächsort zum Besprechungsraum, vom Durchgangsraum zum Präsentationsraum.

Auch der Raum um das Objekt herum ist programmiert und aktiviert. Das Objekt geht eine räumliche Beziehung mit den Räumen der Büros ein. Auf allen Seiten beteiligt sich der umgebende Raum an der mehrdeutigen Nutzung. Auf der Rückseite befindet sich ein Treffpunkt zum Kaffeetrinken in der Korridorzone der Büros, auf der offenen Seite ein Auditorium oder Präsentationsraum als Teil der Büroetage. Im oberen Geschoss gibt es ein Bücherregal und einen Platz zum Lesen oder zum Gedankenaustausch in einem lobbyartigen Raum.

Das Objekt bietet derart viele Möglichkeiten, die von den Nutzenden selbst ausgefüllt werden können. So wie in den Spielplätzen des niederländischen Architekten Aldo van Eyck [Abb. 3], wo eigenständige Objekte zusammen mehrdeutige Übergänge für Kinder und Eltern definieren. Hier können sich alle ihren Platz erobern oder den Raum teilen und gemeinsam spielen oder sich selbst erfinden. Der mehrdeutige Raum im Ebaholz-Projekt lädt zum Treffen, Beobachten, Improvisieren und Reden ein. Eine willkommene Abwechslung zum Büroalltag, in dem Schreibtisch und Computer den Blick und das Sitzen für einen Grossteil des Tages bestimmen.

Handwerk

Die menschliche Dimension spiegelt sich auch in den Verbindungen und Details des Objekts wider. Die Hand des Zimmermanns ist in den Holzverbindungen sichtbar. Man erkennt, wie das Objekt von Menschenhand gefertigt wurde. Die Schwalbenschwanzverbindungen zwischen dem Treppengeländer und den Treppenstufen sowie der Podeste und Wandplatten zeigen die Verbindungsweisen auf traditionelle Art. Die sichtbare Holzmaserung (vertikal und horizontal) verstärkt die Richtung der Elemente der horizontalen Bodenkante und Treppenstufen sowie der vertikalen Wandteile. Die Maserung des Holzes verleiht Atmosphäre und zeigt die Maserung der Bäume. Die vertikale, offene Lattenwand mit den horizontalen Latten, die dazwischen „eingewoben" sind, erzeugt ein transparentes Muster, das an ein Geflecht erinnert.

Die Liebe zum Handwerk ist überall sichtbar. Auf diese Weise tragen die Eingriffe und Details zum menschlichen Erleben, zur Verbindung und zur Inbesitznahme bei. Der Benutzer, die Benutzerin nimmt das Hergestellte mit Aufmerksamkeit wahr. „Ebaholz" hat ein Herz und eine Seele bekommen. Ein Herz, das als zentraler Ort für das Gebäude fungiert, für Bewegung, Begegnung und Gespräche sorgt. Und eine Seele, die dem Büro Menschlichkeit, Wärme, sichtbare Handwerkskunst und Schönheit verleiht.

On the corner of Landstrasse and Fürst-Franz-Josef Strasse in Vaduz stands a seemingly anonymous office building of concrete and glass. A rational grey façade grid reveals the size and scale of the 'office unit'. Each bay in the façade always has a double window with a mid-height transom or a single window with a grey panel adjoining it. The prefabricated façade elements are abstractly detailed. They show little signature of the maker. Although well proportioned, the building looks like a dime a dozen. It lacks a soul, at least on the outside. In contrast to this anonymous façade, students from the University of Liechtenstein have made an intervention in the heart of the building that brings a human size and scale to the building on several levels.

A house within a house

The wooden construction built by the students, with an area of five by five metres and a height of four metres, is a modest and distinctive presence in the middle of the office building. Its volume contains a kitchen, a storage room and chests of drawers. The element provides space for encounters, movement and presentation. The wooden object provides orientation for visitors to the space. It is a landmark in the middle of the building. The stairs and tiered seating connect the first and second floors of the building both spatially and physically.

The intervention creates an intimate space with a human scale that reminds me on the one hand of the room depicted in Albrecht Dürer's *Saint Jerome in His Study* [fig. 1], a wooden volume as a workspace in the middle of a large space. But also the folding house that the artist and filmmaker Jeroen Kooijmans built with students at the Amsterdam Academy of Architecture [fig. 2]: a flexible place for

1   Antonello da Messina, *St Jerome in His Study*, National Gallery, London.

2   Jeroen Kooijmans, artist in residence, Academie van Bouwkunst, Amsterdam, 2010.

3   Spielplatz Zaanhof, Aldo van Eyck, 1953.

The Ebaholz Project and Human Scale

meetings and conversations that openly incorporates the environment.

The intervention fills the heart of the building with a meeting place to sit, hang around, stand and move. Steps to climb the stairs, surfaces to sit on, edges to lean against, a fence to stand against. It defines the interior space. It provides a warm and human scale.

Ambiguous space

The stairs and tiered seating are more than just a vertical connection. The construction houses several practical functions, such as the kitchen worktop on the first floor, the cupboard along the mezzanine above and the storage room and chests of drawers under the tiered seating. But above all, the object creates a place to stay and meet. A place to dwell that is open to reinterpretation and has multiple uses: from place of casual conversation to formal meeting room, from passageway to presentation room.

The space around the object is also programmed and activated. The built element enters into a spatial relationship with the spaces of the university offices. On each side, the surrounding space participates in the ambiguous use. On the back side there is a meeting place where people can drink coffee in the 'corridor zone' of the office, on the open side there is a space for play or presentation as part of the office floor. On the upper floor, the loft has a lobby-like space with a bookcase and a place to read or exchange ideas.

The wooden object offers so many possibilities that can be filled in by the users themselves. As in the playgrounds of Dutch architect Aldo van Eyck [fig. 3], where autonomous objects together define ambiguous transitions for both children and parents. Here, everyone can conquer their place or share space and play together or invent themselves.

The ambiguous space in Ebaholz invites people to meet, observe, improvise and talk. This is a welcome addition to office life, where the desks and computers determine the atmosphere and people sit for much of the day.

Craft

The human dimension is also reflected in the connections and details of the object. The carpenter's hand is evident in the wood joints. You can see how the object was made by human hands. The dovetail joints between the stair railing and the stair tread, and between the tiered seating and wall parts, illustrate the traditional method of joining. The visible wood grain (vertical and horizontal) reinforces the direction of various elements, such as vertical walls and horizontal floor edges and stair treads. The grain of the wood adds atmosphere and reveals the grain of the trees. The open wall of vertical slats with interwoven horizontal slats creates a translucent pattern, like a net curtain.

The love of making is visible everywhere. In this way, the built object and its details contribute to the human experience, connection and ownership. The user embraces what has been made with care. Ebaholz has been given a heart and a soul. A heart that functions as a central place for the building, providing movement, meeting and conversation. And a soul that brings humanity to the office with warmth, visible craftsmanship and humane beauty.

Die Weichheit des Holzes — Das konstruierte Material für konstruierte Räume

The Softness of Wood — A Constructed Material for Constructed Spaces

Mario Rinke

Holz gilt als Inbegriff der Nachhaltigkeit bei der Wahl von Baustoffen, und doch sind die Schwierigkeiten gross, es im breiten aktuellen Baudiskurs auf internationaler Ebene zu verankern. Und selbst wenn das Bekenntnis zum Holzbau etabliert ist, warum sprechen wir heute vom Holz, das seine Nachhaltigkeit beweisen muss? Weil Holz schon lange nicht mehr nur das gewachsene, unschuldige Holz ist, sondern sich in einer Reihe industrieller Produkte einordnet. Holz kann dabei dann für massive, permanente Funktionen wie das Tragskelett oder für leichte, vergleichsweise temporäre Funktionen wie die Verkleidung oder das Mobiliar eingesetzt werden. Und gerade hier liegt der Unterschied: Der traditionelle Baustoff Holz wird im modernen, industriellen Kontext nicht mehr nur einfach eingesetzt, sondern es wird gerade für diese Orte, Funktionen, ja Einsatzdauern gefertigt. In diesem Essay soll in aller Kürze eine Übersicht gegeben werden, wie das Holz historisch zum konstruierten Material wurde und wie es sich heute, über seine natürliche Beschaffenheit hinaus, sinnvoll im Sinne einer zirkulären Architektur einsetzen lassen kann.

So lange Holz als Konstruktionsmaterial im Bauen eingesetzt wurde, so lange spielte auch die praktische Fertigung im Konstruktionsprozess eine Rolle. Das Konstruieren beinhaltete neben dem notwendigen Fügen der einzelnen Teile auch das Formen der Teile selbst. Die Trennung von Bearbeitung, also dem Abbund, und Montage der Komponenten hat im Holzbau eine lange Geschichte und so differenzierte Formen von handwerklichen Praktiken hervorgebracht, die sich lokal mitunter stark unterscheiden. Dabei hat sich auch der Fokus der Bearbeitung durch den Holzbetrieb verändert. Aus Gründen der Verfügbarkeit von langen oder geraden Hölzern, deren hohen Kosten oder auch wegen teils fehlender technischer Kenntnisse wurden in der Konstruktionsgeschichte jahrhundertelang Bauteile aus kleinen Holzstücken zusammengesetzt. Als Entwicklungslinie bis heute vollzieht sich das Zusammensetzen dabei auf zwei Ebenen. Einerseits werden Tragglieder gebildet, die zahlreiche Einzelteile zusammenfassen. Anderseits bilden sich durch das Zusammenfügen kompakte, präzise Objekte die vor allem in der modularen Wiederholung zum Einsatz kommen.

Geschichtete und verschränkte Bauteile

Schon für die Antike wird das präzise Zusammenfügen zu grossen oder besonders geformten Bauteilen beschrieben. Walter Sackur (1871–1926) zeigt 1925 in seiner Untersuchung zur bautechnischen Literatur des Altertums, wie durch Stapelung von einzelnen Balken massive Kranmasten oder besonders robuste Dachstühle hergestellt werden.

Vor allem grosse Brücken- und Dachtragwerke werden kunstvoll und präzise aus kurzen Bauteilen gefertigt. Teilweise werden komplexe Bogenformen von Brücken auch auf Dächer übertragen. Sebastiano Serlio (1475–1554) beschreibt in seinem Architekturtraktat mögliche Zierformen der Dächer, die wiederum weitestgehend auf französischen Bauweisen beruhen. Traditionellerweise, so erklärt er, stellen diese Dächer Dreiecksformen dar, die aus einzelnen Holzstäben je nach Spannweite gebildet werden [Abb. 1]. Zur Überdeckung grosser Säle könne man aber auch auf die elegante Variante der verschränkten, gekrümmten Hölzer zurückgreifen, die Serlio nur darstellt und leider nicht weiter beschreibt.[1]

Die konstruktive Erfindung, einen Bogen aus relativ kurzen überlappenden Holzstücken

Wood is seen as the epitome of sustainability when it comes to the choice of building material, and yet it is very difficult to anchor it in the broad contemporary international discourse on construction. And even though the commitment to wood construction is well established, why are we now talking about wood having to prove its sustainability? Wood is no longer just the innocent wood that was simply grown; it is now part of a range of industrial products. Wood can hence be used for solid, permanent functions such as the load-bearing frame of a building, or for lightweight and comparatively temporary functions such as cladding or furniture. And this is precisely where the difference lies: the traditional building material wood is no longer simply used in a modern, industrial context, but is manufactured precisely for these places, functions and even periods of use. This essay will provide a very brief overview of how wood has historically evolved into a constructed material and how it can be used today in meaningful ways that support the interests of circular architecture and go beyond its natural properties.

For as long as wood has been used as a building material, its practical production has also played a role in the construction process. In addition to the necessary joining of individual parts, the construction process also involved the shaping of the parts themselves. The separation of processing (i.e. the conversion of raw timber into dimensional lumber) from component assembly has a long history in timber construction and has given rise to a diversity of skilled practices, some of which vary widely within a local area. The focus of processing by the timber company has also changed. Due to the limited availability of long or straight timber, its high cost, or a lack of technical knowledge, building components have been assembled from small pieces of wood for centuries in the history of construction. As a line of development leading up to the present day, assembly takes place at two levels. On the one hand, structural elements are created that consist of numerous individual parts. On the other hand, joining them together creates compact, precise objects that are mainly used in modular repetition.

Stacked and interlocked components

The precise joining of parts to form large or specially shaped components has been described since ancient times. In 1925, Walter Sackur (1871–1926), in his study of ancient construction literature, showed how massive crane masts or particularly strong roof structures were made by stacking individual beams.

In particular, large bridge and roof structures were elaborately and precisely constructed from short components. In some cases, the complex arch shapes of bridges were also applied to roofs. In his treatise on architecture, Sebastiano Serlio (1475¬1554) describes possible decorative forms for roofs, which in turn were largely based on French construction methods. Traditionally, he explains, these roofs were triangular in shape, formed from individual wooden members that varied according to the span [fig. 1]. To span large halls, however, the elegant option of interlocking curved timbers could be used, which Serlio only illustrates, unfortunately without any further description.[1]

The structural innovation of assembling an arch from relatively short, overlapping pieces of wood can be traced back to Philibert de L'Orme (c. 1510–1570). A technical writer on stone masonry and vaulting techniques, he

zusammenzusetzen, geht auf Philibert de L'Orme (ca. 1510–1570) zurück. Als Fachautor für Steinmetz- und Gewölbetechniken stellt er diese Methode 1561 in einer Schrift zu baulichen Erfindungen dar.[2] David Gilly (1748–1808) greift die Bauweise später wieder auf, die bis dahin nur eine Randerscheinung in der Bautechnik darstellt, und bewirbt die Bohlendächer 1797 in einer gesonderten Publikation. Ebenso wie de L'Orme sah Gilly den häufigen Mangel an grossem Bauholz als Hauptgrund für eine Bildung von Holzbögen aus kleinen schwachen Stücken.

Interessanterweise stammt die wichtigste technische Neuerung des industriellen Holzbaus aus dem Schreinerhandwerk: Der Zimmermeister Otto Hetzer (1846–1911) aus Weimar war vor allem im Innenausbau tätig und trieb dort verfeinerte, kleinteilige Konstruktionstechniken voran, die sich in zahlreichen Patenten niederschlugen. Sein 1906 patentiertes „gebogenes Holzbauteil", DRP 197773 [Abb. 2], zielte aber auf Dachkonstruktionen und markierte den Beginn einer sehr erfolgreichen Holzbauunternehmung und — weit darüber hinaus — eine Zeitenwende im Holzbau hin zum Brettschichtholz, einer grossformatigen, ganz eigenständigen Industriebauweise.[3] Diese neue Technologie war dort erfolgreich, wo grosse Holzformate oder Stahl knapp und teuer waren. Gerade der Erste Weltkrieg bescherte dem modernen Holzbau einen grossen Schub. Vielerorts ersetzte Holz wegen des Eisen- und Kohlemangels den Stahl, oft sogar in der gleichen Form und Typologie.[4] Hinzu kamen andere Bestrebungen, etwa der Rückgriff auf lokale Ressourcen und lokale handwerklich-konstruktive Traditionen — die zentralen Aspekte heutiger Holzpolitik.[5] Beides stand bereits bei der Renaissance des Holzes vor über hundert Jahren im Zentrum.

Geschichtete und gereihte Module

Das noch viel kleinteiligere Fügen von Holz mit Furnieren ist bereits sehr alt und kann bis ins alte Ägypten zurückverfolgt werden. Für das moderne Bauwesen spielt das Sperrholz erst in der Mitte des 20. Jahrhunderts eine Rolle. Die ersten industriellen Schritte, mit den Patenten von John Henry Belter 1858 und John K. Mayo 1868, zeigen das Streben nach einem günstigen Ersatz von komplexen Konstruktionen aus vielen Teilen [Abb. 3], das zugleich eine besonders kunstvolle Form oder Oberfläche ermöglichte.[6]

Neben der Entwicklung von Holzwerkstoffen lässt sich im 20. Jahrhundert aber eine zunehmend radikalere Trennung von Bearbeitung und Montage der Komponenten erkennen, aus der wiederum differenzierte Formen von industriellen Praktiken und Produkten entstanden. Dabei veränderte sich auch der Schwerpunkt der Bearbeitung durch die Holzbetriebe: weg von einzelnen komplexen Teilen hin zu Modulen, die präzise und günstig zusammengeführt werden. Schon der frühe Ständerbau und der komplexere Fachwerkbau waren als streng schematische Systeme organisiert, die durch die Ordnung der Teile mit klarer Hierarchie und jeweiliger Repetition die Gesamtkonstruktion in Werkstattproduktion und Montage trennten. Das Raster bestimmte sowohl die Länge der Teile als auch ihre Position.

Am sichtbarsten ist diese Ordnung als architektonisches Prinzip im traditionellen japanischen Holzbau.[7] Die lokal genormten Bauteilformen und das Grundmass des Skelettbaus ermöglichten nicht nur eine annähernd katalogmässige Fertigung, sondern auch eine relativ einfache Wartung und Reparatur. Wie sehr das handwerkliche Wissen im Umgang mit

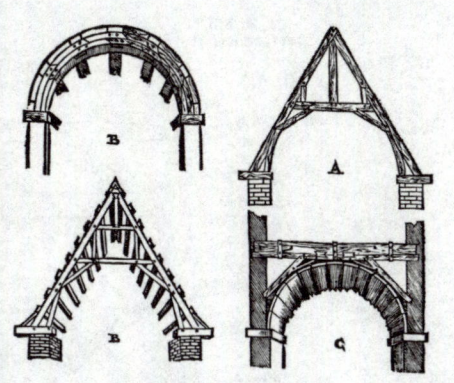

1 Dachkonstruktionen bei Sebastiano Serlio (Serlio 2001). Roof structures by Sebastiano Serlio (Serlio 2001).

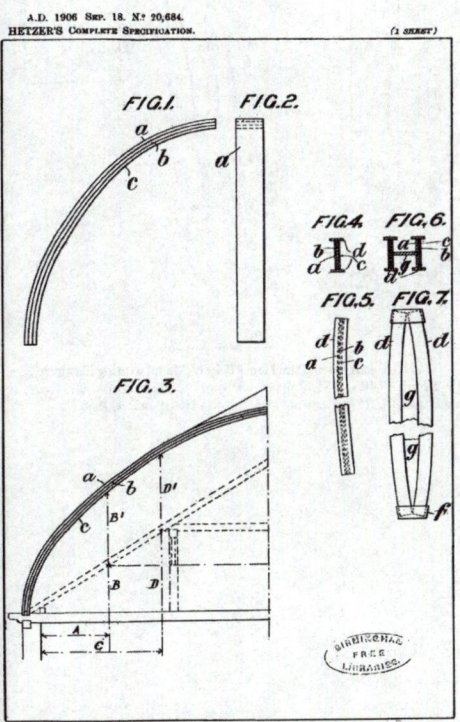

2 Ersatz des Holzdachstuhls durch bogenförmige Elemente, DRP 197773, Otto Hetzer, 1906. Replacement of wooden roof framing with arched elements, German patent no. 197773, Otto Hetzer, 1906.

described this method in 1561 in a treatise on architectural inventions.[2] David Gilly (1748–1808) later revisited this method of construction, which had previously been a marginal phenomenon in building techniques, and promoted the plank roofs in a dedicated publication of his own in 1797. Like de L'Orme, Gilly saw the frequent lack of large timbers as the main reason for constructing wooden arches from small, weak pieces.

Interestingly, the most important technical innovation in industrial timber construction came from the carpentry trade: The master carpenter Otto Hetzer (1846–1911) from Weimar, whose work focused mainly on interiors, refined detailed techniques for interior construction, many of which were reflected in numerous patents. However, his 'gebogenes Holzbauteil'; Patent 197773 [fig. 2], patented in 1906, was intended for roof construction and marked the beginning of a highly successful timber construction business and, far more importantly, a historic shift in wood construction to glue-laminated timber (glulam), an entirely unique, large-format industrial construction method.[3] This new technology was successful where large-dimension timber and/or steel was scarce and expensive. The First World War in particular gave modern timber construction a major boost. In many places, due to shortages of iron and coal, timber replaced steel, often with no change in form or typology.[4] Other aspirations also emerged, such as a renewed reliance on local resources, local skills and local building traditions—the central aspects of today's timber policy.[5] Both were at the heart of the timber renaissance over a hundred years ago.

Holz durch ein radikal einfaches System abgelöst werden kann, zeigt der amerikanische Ständerbau, das sogenannte Balloon- und Platform-Framing. Der Mangel an gut ausgebildeten Bauleuten führte dabei zu einer starken Vereinfachung der Konstruktionsweise der aus Europa gut bekannten Ständerbauweise. Die Bauteile wurden vereinheitlicht, indem für die Wände vertikal durchlaufende dünne Pfosten mit einem standardisierten Querschnitt verwendet wurden, angeordnet in immer gleichen Abständen.[8] Möglich machten diese massenhaft eingesetzte Bauweise vor allem leistungsstarke und präzise wasserkraftbetriebene Sägewerke zur schnellen und günstigen Verarbeitung der Baumstämme sowie die industrielle Fertigung von Nägeln.

Industrieller Holzmodulbau

Als zu Beginn des 20. Jahrhunderts das Brettschichtholz international an Einfluss gewann, wurden bereits kleine, mobile Gebäude mit Modulen vorgefertigt. Eines der führenden europäischen Unternehmen für komplett vorgefertigte Gebäude aus Holz war Christoph & Unmack aus Niesky in der deutschen Oberlausitz. Ausgehend von einem erworbenen Patent zur Herstellung mobiler Militärbaracken, wuchs die Firma vor allem durch die erfolgreiche massenhafte Entwicklung von standardisierten Wohnbauten für die britischen Kolonien.[9] Der deutsche Architekt Konrad Wachsmann, der Ende der 1920er-Jahre für Christoph & Unmack als Chefarchitekt deren Produktpalette verbreiterte, entwickelte nach seiner Emigration in die USA zusammen mit dem ebenfalls emigrierten Walter Gropius ein rationales, elementiertes und transportables Wohngebäude, das „Packaged House System".

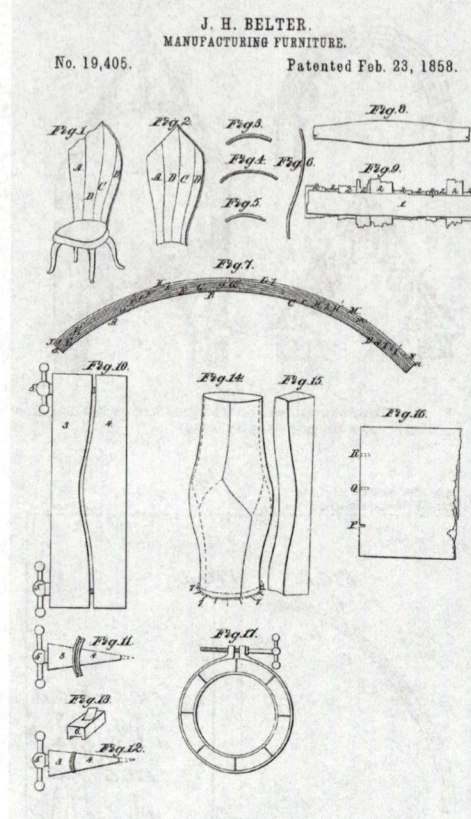

3   U.S.-Patent von John Henry Belter, „Manufacturing Furniture", U.S.-Patent 19,405, 1858. 'Improvement in the Method of Manufacturing Furniture', US patent no. 19,405, John Henry Belter, 1858.

Stacked and arrayed modules

The much finer joining of wood veneers is already very old and can be traced back to ancient Egypt. Plywood did not play a role in modern construction until the middle of the 20th century. The first industrial steps, with the patents of John Henry Belter in 1858 [fig. 3] and John K. Mayo in 1868, show the desire to find an inexpensive substitute for complex constructions consisting of many parts, while at the same time providing a particularly artistic form or surface.[6]

In addition to the development of engineered wood materials, the 20th century also saw an increasingly radical separation between the processing and assembly of components, which in turn gave rise to differentiated industrial practices and products. This also changed the focus of processing by the timber companies, away from individual complex parts and towards modules that could be assembled accurately and inexpensively. Even the early post-and-beam structures and the more complex half-timbered buildings were organised as strictly schematic systems with a clear hierarchy of repetitive parts, allowing the overall construction process to be divided into workshop production and on-site assembly. The grid determined both the length of the parts and their positions.

This ordering system is most visible as an architectural principle in traditional Japanese timber construction.[7] The locally standardised component shapes and basic dimensions of the skeletal frame enabled not only near-catalogue production but also relatively simple maintenance and repair. The extent to which the knowledge of woodworking skills could be replaced by a radically simple system is demonstrated by the American stud construction methods known as balloon framing and platform framing. The lack of well-trained builders led to a great simplification of the familiar European post-and beam construction. The components for the walls were made consistent by using thin, vertically continuous posts with a standardised cross-section, always placed at uniform intervals.[8] This method of construction, now employed on a massive scale, was made possible chiefly by the availability of powerful and accurate water-powered sawmills that could process logs quickly and inexpensively, and by the industrial production of nails.

Industrial modular timber construction

As glulam began to gain international acceptance in the early 20th century, small, mobile buildings were already being prefabricated with modules. One of the leading European manufacturers of fully prefabricated timber buildings was Christoph & Unmack, based in Niesky in the Upper Lusatia region of Germany. Starting with a patent it had acquired for the production of mobile military barracks, the company grew primarily through the successful mass development of standardised housing for the British colonies.[9] After emigrating to the USA, the German architect Konrad Wachsmann — who had expanded Christoph & Unmack's product range as its chief architect in the late 1920s — developed a rational, modular and transportable dwelling, the 'Packaged House' system, together with Walter Gropius, who had also emigrated to the USA.

They used wood, a light and abundant building material, and applied the extensive knowledge of panelised construction that Wachsmann had gained from his work at Christoph

Sie griffen auf den leichten und reichlich verfügbaren Baustoff Holz zurück und verwendeten das Konstruktionswissen der Tafelbauweise, das Wachsmann aus seiner Tätigkeit bei Christoph & Unmack gut kannte. Für ihr eigenes Paneelsystem entwickelten Wachsmann und Gropius den Tafelbau weiter und generierten Module, die zur eigentlichen Grammatik des Konstruierens und Entwerfens werden sollten. Im Werk ihrer Firma General Panel Corporation konnte das Holz schnell und präzise für diese Zwecke verarbeitet und zu modularen Wandelementen gefügt werden, fertig ausgestattet mit Beschlägen und Glasfüllungen.[10] Diese immer gleichen Paneele, gefertigt innerhalb von zwei Stunden, konnten auf der Baustelle innerhalb eines Tages zusammengesetzt werden. Es war eine Konstruktionsweise nahe an der heutigen Holzbaupraxis—sogar radikaler, denn sie hatte einen universellen Anspruch: Die Module sollten nicht nur günstig verfügbar und für verschiedene Bauformen und Funktionen einsetzbar sein, sondern sich auch bei späteren Umbauten ändern und wiederverwenden lassen. Die Bauweise zielte also auf ein offenes System. Um die einzelnen Teile verbinden und auch wieder voneinander lösen zu können, entwarf Wachsmann mehrere Versionen eines universellen Metallknotens, der jeweils in die Holzpaneele eingelassen war. Das Projekt war für eine individualisierte Massengesellschaft gedacht, scheiterte allerdings bereits nach wenigen Jahren aufgrund zu geringer Nachfrage.

Extreme des heutigen Holzbaus

Das geformte Grossbauteil und das multifunktionale Modul — das sind die beiden hochtechnisierten Extreme des heutigen Holzbaus, die mit präziser und komplexer Vorfertigung auf eine einfache und schnelle Montage abzielen: Das industrielle Brettschichtholz ist ohnehin auf eine gewisse Vorfertigung angewiesen und wird im Werk entsprechend der Zielgeometrie gekrümmt oder mit spezifischem, möglicherweise variierendem Querschnitt gefertigt; der Abbund mit digital gesteuerter Fräse schafft die notwendige Geometrie, um das Teil später passgenau einbauen zu können. Andererseits wird in den im Werk fabrizierten seriellen Tafelmodulen, ausgestattet mit Dämmung, Fenstern und Versorgungssträngen, das Haus als Mikrokosmos abgebildet.[11] Neben der Verfeinerung neuer Holzwerkstoffe liegt gerade hierin die Wertschöpfung für die Holzbetriebe. Von den einfachen Holzelementen der Christoph-&-Unmack-Kataloghäuser über Wachsmanns Paneelsystem bis zu den hochausgerüsteten Modulen heute—der Holzbau entwickelt sich hin zu immer umfangreicheren, massgeschneiderten Produkten.

Anhand der in diesem Buch vorgestellten Arbeiten im Innenausbau im „Ebaholz" lässt sich aber auch gut die Verschränkung von heutiger Materialproduktion, Handwerk und Moduldenken beobachten. Die Treppenmöbel aus verleimten Eschenstäben wurden zu einer präzisen und spezifischen Landschaft zusammengefügt, während die manuell gefügten Wände aus massiven, industriell gefertigten Weisstannenplatten hergestellt und in der Werkstatt konfektioniert wurden.

Zirkuläres Holz

Der Einsatz von Holz statt Beton oder Stahl kann nicht der einzige Beitrag zu einer nachhaltigeren Baukultur sein. Denn selbst wenn wir nur aus Holz bauen wollten, würden die bestehenden Ressourcen nicht ausreichen,

& Unmack. For their own panel system, Wachsmann and Gropius developed panelised construction further, creating modules that were to become the intrinsic grammar of construction and design. At the factory of their company, General Panel Corporation, the wood could be processed quickly and accurately processed and assembled into modular wall units, complete with fittings and glazing.[10] These panels, which were always identical, were fabricated within two hours and could be assembled on the building site within a day. It was a construction method very similar to today's timber construction—but even more radical, because it had a universal claim: the modules should not only be available at low cost and suitable for different building forms and functions, but should also be able to be modified and reused in subsequent renovations and conversions. The construction method therefore aimed to be an open system. Wachsmann designed several versions of a universal metal connector that was embedded in each of the wooden panels in order to enable the individual parts to be joined and later separated. The project was intended for an individualised mass society but failed within a few years due to insufficient demand.

The extremes of contemporary timber construction

The large-scale component formed component and the multifunctional module—these are the two high-tech extremes of today's timber construction, aimed at easy and quick assembly through precise and complex prefabrication: Industrial glulam already relies on a degree of prefabrication, and is bent in the factory to achieve the target geometry of the curved form or produced with a specific, possibly varying cross-section; trimming with a digitally controlled milling machine creates the geometry necessary to install the part with a precise fit later. On the other hand, the factory-produced, serialised panel modules, fitted with insulation, windows and utility lines, represent the house as a microcosm.[11] Alongside the refinement of new engineered wood products, this is precisely where the added value for timber companies lies. From the simple wooden elements of the Christoph & Unmack catalogue houses to Wachsmann's panel system and today's highly equipped modules—timber construction is evolving into ever more extensive and specially equipped customised products.

The interior woodwork in Ebaholz presented in this book is a good example of how modern material production, craft and modular thinking are intertwined. The staircase furniture elements, made of glued ash slats, were joined together to form a precise and specific landscape, while the manually assembled walls were made of solid, industrially produced panels of silver fir, fabricated in the workshop.

Circular wood

Contributions to a more sustainable building culture cannot be limited to using wood instead of concrete or steel. Even if we wanted to build exclusively with wood, the available resources would not be sufficient, even in forest-rich regions. So let us be clear: Not every timber building is a sustainable building! We need to consider wood intended for use in timber structures as a future resource of equal value to wood harvested directly from the forest. The 'softness' of wood has always made it a manageable and relevant building material throughout

nicht einmal in waldreichen Regionen. Deshalb muss klar werden: Nicht jedes Holzgebäude ist ein nachhaltiges Gebäude! Wir müssen das Holz für den Entwurf von Holzbauwerken ebenso als zukünftige Resource begreifen wie das Holz direkt aus dem Wald. Die „Weichheit" des Holzes hat es zu einem in der Konstruktionsgeschichte immer handhabbaren und relevanten Baumaterial gemacht. Heute sollten wir die daraus entwickelten Holzprodukte und -bauteile „weich" einsetzen. Entsprechend müssten die Bauteile, die wir aus Holz konstruieren, der Stabilität seiner Funktion entsprechen. Das heisst, je kurzlebiger die Funktionsschicht des Bauteils ist, desto einfacher entnehmbar und wiederverwendbar sollte es sein. Wenn der moderne Holzbau gerade seine Stärken in der schnellen und einfachen Montage hat, warum dann nicht auch in seiner Demontage?

Das enge Zusammenführen von Tragwerk, Fassade und Versorgung in möglichst kompakten Modulen steht im Widerspruch zur Nachhaltigkeitsforschung, die deren klare räumliche Trennung fordert [Abb. 4].[12] Die einzelnen Funktionsebenen haben sehr unterschiedliche Lebenszyklen und müssen deshalb einfach zu erreichen sein. Module können für die Planung und Montage als Pakete gedacht werden, müssen aber offene Systeme bleiben. Im Sinne einer zirkulären Architektur sollten sich Module des modernen Holzbaus, erstens, nach ihrem Einsatz ganz oder teilweise in einem anderen Gebäude verwenden lassen, was eine einfache Demontage und eine unkomplizierte Sanierung des Moduls voraussetzt. Damit rückt die Fügung der Teile wieder mehr in den Blickpunkt. In jedem Fall aber sollten, zweitens, die Materialbestandteile eines Moduls einfach zu trennen sein, wenn diese in ihre Materialkreisläufe zurückgeführt werden sollen. Gleiches

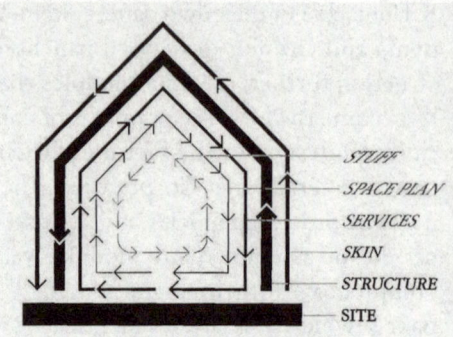

4   Diagramm der Funktionsschichten eines Gebäudes, Dicke je nach Veränderungsgeschwindigkeit, nach Frank Duffy auch „Shearing Layer" genannt, aus: Stewart Brand, „How Buildings Learn: What Happens After They're Built", 1994. Diagram of the functional layers of a building, with their thickness depending on the rate of change; termed 'shearing layers' by Frank Duffy. Source: Stewart Brand, *How Buildings Learn: What Happens After They're Built* (New York: Viking, 1994).

the history of construction. In today's world, we should use the wood products and components developed from this wood in a 'soft' way. Consequently, the components we make from wood should match the stability of the functions of these products and components. This means that the more transient the functional layer of the component, the easier it should be to remove and reuse. If the strength of modern timber construction lies in its in quick and easy assembly, why not also in its disassembly?

The close integration of load-bearing structure, façade and services in modules that are as compact as possible contradicts sustainability research, which calls for their clear spatial separation[12] [fig. 4]. The discrete functional levels have very different life cycles and therefore need to be easily accessible. For the purposes of planning and assembly, modules can be conceived as packages, but they must remain open systems. In the spirit of circular architecture, modern timber construction modules should, firstly, be able to be reused, in whole or in part, in another building after their initial use, which presupposes easy dismantling and uncomplicated refurbishment of the module. This puts the focus back on the joining of the parts. Secondly, the material components of a module should, in any case, always be easy to separate if they are to be returned to their material cycles. The same applies to massive load-bearing components. Of course, with today's production methods they could be given special shapes. However, in the spirit of cascading resource use, where downcycling is slowed as much as possible, it should be possible to use the compact wood mass as a raw material for subsequent components. Thirdly, as an overriding principle, timber buildings should be designed in such a way that they can be easily adapted for other uses.

These three requirements of circularity, at the material, component and building levels, are also placed on all other construction methods and materials, now and in the near future.[13] In the long historical perspective, and especially in the context of rapid industrial development, it is evident that not only have construction methods changed, but above all the role of components in construction as a whole has changed. Shifting the focus from the configuration of parts to the configured material is a hallmark of constructive modernism. The impetus was particularly strong as economic pressures dictated efficient methods of construction. Where are ecological pressures pushing us? The strategic use of wood in accordance with its inherent material mobility[14] in the life cycle of a building, with constant repair and repurposing and thus constant alterations and continued construction, invites us to think not only about spatiality but also about temporality. It brings us back to the configuration of parts, not so much in order to create complex components, but rather to create a building that is appropriate to its inherent functionality, both in terms of space and period of use.

gilt für massive, tragende Bauteile. Sie könnten selbstverständlich im Sinne heutiger Fertigungsmethoden spezifisch geformt sein. Nur sollte die kompakte Holzmasse als Rohstoff für spätere Bauteile verwendet werden können, ganz im Sinne der kaskadischen Resourcennutzung durch ein möglichst langsames Downcycling. Als übergeordnetes Prinzip sollten, drittens, Holzbauten so konzipiert sein, dass sie ohne grossen Aufwand umzunutzen sind.

Diese drei Anforderungen der Zirkularität auf Material-, Bauteil- und Gebäudeebene werden auch an alle anderen Bauweisen und -materialien gestellt, jetzt und in naher Zukunft.[13] In der langen geschichtlichen Betrachtung, vor allem in der schnellen industriellen Entwicklung, zeigt sich nicht nur ein Wandel der Konstruktionsweisen, sondern vor allem ein Wandel der Rolle des Bauteils in der Gesamtkonstruktion. Die Verschiebung des Fokus weg von der Konfiguration der Teile hin zum konfigurierten Material ist ein Kennzeichen der konstruktiven Moderne. Der Schub war besonders stark, als wirtschaftlicher Druck zu effizienten Bauweisen zwang. Wohin schiebt uns der ökologische Druck? Das strategische Nutzen von Holz entsprechend seiner natürlichen Mobilität[14] im Lebenszyklus des Bauwerks mit permanenter Reparatur und Umnutzung und folglich einem stetigen Um- und Weiterbauen lädt ein, neben der Räumlichkeit auch immer die Zeitlichkeit mitzudenken. Es bringt uns wieder zu einem Konfigurieren der Teile, und zwar weniger untereinander zu komplexen Bauteilen, sondern zum Bauwerk entsprechend seiner eigenen Funktion im Raum und in der Verwendungszeit.

Prototypen Wandsystem Prototypes wall system

Prototypen Wandsystem Prototypes wall system

Prototypen Wandsystem Prototypes wall system

Prozess oder Produkt —
Über die Komplexität
handwerklicher
Unterrichtsmethoden im
Architekturstudium

Process or Product —
On the Complexity of
Practical Teaching Methods
in Architectural Studies

Wolfgang Schwarzmann
Livia Herle

Einen eigenen Entwurf tatsächlich umzusetzen, ist vielen Studierenden während der Architekturausbildung (noch) nicht möglich. Die im Unterricht aufgeworfenen Fragestellungen basieren auf fiktiven Aufgaben und werden meist nur auf dem Papier oder am Modell erforscht. Um den Studierenden aber bereits in der Ausbildung ein Gefühl für Baustoffe, handwerkliche Prozesse und ein entsprechend erweitertes Verständnis zwischen Entwurf und Ausführung zu ermöglichen, sind Hochschulen bestrebt, auch Projekte mit realem Output einzubinden. Das im Rahmen dieser Publikation vorgestellte Ebaholz-Projekt der Uni Liechtenstein beleuchtet einen solchen 1:1-Prozess über die Dauer von einem Semester. Der folgende Artikel diskutiert die Fragestellung, inwiefern ein solches Vorhaben die Ausbildung der Studierenden beeinflusst, welche Anpassung in der Lehre damit verbunden ist und ob der Unterricht letztlich einer Projekt- oder Prozessorientierung angepasst werden muss [Abb. 1].

Die Planungsaufgaben von Architektinnen und Architekten stellen sich gleichermassen aus Theorie und Praxis zusammen. Gewerkeübergreifend arbeiten sie als „Generalisten", wobei sie sich Wissen in allen Fachgebieten des Bausektors aneignen müssen. Diese vielfältigen Ansprüche an zukünftige Planende stellt die Ausbildung vor viele Anforderungen. Neben theoretischem Wissen in Entwurf und Raumgefüge, aber auch Baukultur und Städtebau darf das Konstruieren und ein Gespür für Baustoffe nicht zu kurz kommen. Um hier sowohl theoretische Grundlagen als auch praktische Fähigkeiten in der Ausbildung zu vermitteln, zeigen sich tatsächlich im Masstab 1:1 umgesetzte Projekte immer wieder als geeignete Methoden. Studierende sind dabei angehalten, ihre Entwürfe sowohl planerisch auszuarbeiten, als auch Teile davon eigenhändig umzusetzen.

Während in der Architekturlehre an Hochschulen immer ein starker Bezug zur Praxis, zur realen Welt und zu Baustoffen gesucht wird, lassen sich jedoch gerade diese Strategien zur Bewertung einer Leistung in die Architekturausbildung nur sehr begrenzt übersetzen. Wird im späteren beruflichen Alltag ein starker Fokus auf die Qualität des finalen Ergebnisses, das präsentierte Produkt gelegt, so muss gerade in der Architekturausbildung auch eine Gewichtung auf die Lernkurve, also den eigentlichen Prozess, gelegt werden. Diese erweiterte Vielfalt in der Lehre bringt jedoch nicht nur zusätzliche Lehrinhalte auf handwerklicher und materieller Ebene für die Studierenden, sondern bedarf auch einer grundlegenden Ausrichtung der Lernziele und Beurteilungsmodalitäten. Gestellte Aufgaben könnten so aus didaktischer Sicht zwischen einer prozessorientierten oder produktorientieren Herangehensweise differenziert werden.

Beim produktorientierten Arbeiten wird der Fokus auf das Endprodukt gelegt. In der Regel wird die Benotung zu einer Vorlesung, Übung oder eines Seminares am Ende des Semesters über eine Leistungsabfrage bewerkstelligt. Im besten Fall können die Studierenden anhand einer Prüfungsabfrage oder durch das Verfassen einer Seminararbeit vorweisen, dass sie die vermittelten Inhalte verstanden haben und widerspiegeln können. Ein vorgeschalteter Lernprozess kommt durch eine abschliessende Prüfung zu einer Note. Für Planende entspricht diese Situation einem klassischen Architekturwettbewerb, bei dem nach einer mehrwöchigen Arbeitsphase ein Projekt durch die Jury gewertet wird. In diesem Fall kann von einer sehr produktorientierten

Gewichtung gesprochen werden, da in letzter Konsequenz „nur" der finale Entwurf, das Ergebnis auf einem Plakat, bewertet wird.

Bei prozessorientiertem Arbeiten kann im Gegensatz dazu der Fokus bereits auf die ersten Arbeitsschritte ab der Ausgabe einer Übung gelegt werden. Studierende skizzieren, planen und bauen Modelle in verschiedenen Massstäben, sie entwickeln Prototypen und haben hierfür bis zuletzt den Spielraum, verschiedensten Gedankengängen nachzugehen. Ein wesentlicher Unterschied zur produktorientierten Arbeitsweise ist der Aspekt, dass all diese Zwischenschritte später ebenfalls ein integraler Bestandteil der präsentierten Arbeit sind. Die dabei im Prozess entstehenden Produkte wie Skizzen, Modelle und 1:1-Prototypen müssen dazu jedoch genauestens ausgewählt und dokumentiert werden, um später wieder als Teil der Geschichte, des Prozesses vorgezeigt werden zu können.

1 Möbelbauprozess während der „Maak Week" in Antwerpen, März 2024. Furniture construction process during 'Maak Week' in Antwerp, March 2024.

Diese Kombination aus der Erstellung planerischer Grundlagen und der folgenden handwerklichen Umsetzung ist an der Architekturuniversität in Antwerpen im Curriculum verankert. Im Rahmen der Lehrveranstaltung „Spatial Tectonics; Studio Architectonisch Ontwerp 1:1" unter der Anleitung von Prof. Mario Rinke (UANTWERP), Leen De Brabandere (UANTWERP) und Alessandro Tellini (ETH Zurich) wurden die Studierenden während eines Semesters mit der Entwicklung und Herstellung von Holzmöbelstücken beauftragt. Organisiert als Gruppenarbeiten wurde über die Dauer von vier Wochen ein zugeteilter Stellplatz auf dem Campus der Universität Antwerpen oder in einem der Museen der Stadt analysiert, mögliche Konstruktionslösungen erarbeitet sowie erste Prototypen hergestellt.

Many students (still) rarely have the opportunity to actually build their own designs during their architectural studies. The issues raised in an educational setting are based on fictitious tasks and are usually explored only on paper or through models. However, in order to give students a feel for building materials and technical processes, and a correspondingly broader understanding of the link between design and execution, universities also strive to incorporate projects with real physical output. The University of Liechtenstein's Ebaholz project, presented in this publication, illustrates such a one-to-one scale undertaking over the course of a semester. The following article discusses the extent to which such an endeavour influences the education of students, what adjustments need to be made to the teaching curriculum and whether teaching activities ultimately need to be adapted to reflect an orientation toward project or process [fig. 1].

The planning tasks of professional architects consist of equal parts theory and practice. They work as 'generalists' across all trades and must acquire knowledge in all fields of specialisation within the construction sector. These diverse demands on future planning professionals present challenges for the academic curriculum. Along with theoretical knowledge in design and spatial composition, not to mention building culture and urban design, it is important not to neglect construction and a feel for building materials. In order to impart both theoretical principles and practical skills during education, projects that are actually realised at full scale have repeatedly proven to be an effective method. Students are encouraged not only to develop their designs using conventional planning methods, but also to actually build parts of them themselves.

While architectural education in universities always strives for a strong connection to professional practice, the real world and building materials, these strategies for assessing performance can only be translated to a very limited extent into the architecture training. If the quality of the end result—the presented product—is of paramount importance in later professional life, then it is all the more important that architectural education also emphasises the learning curve, the actual process leading to the product. However, this expanded range of teaching methods not only provides students with additional teaching additional content in terms of craft and materials, but also requires a fundamental alignment of learning objectives and assessment modalities. Thus, from a didactic point of view, one might differentiate between approaches that are process-oriented versus product-oriented.

In product-oriented work, the focus is placed on the end product. As a rule, the grading for a lecture, exercise or seminar is done at the end of the semester by means of a performance assessment. In the best case, students will be able to demonstrate that they have understood the material and can communicate it correctly, for example by taking an examination or writing a seminar paper. A previous learning process is graded by means of a final exam. The equivalent situation for planning professionals is a classic architectural competition in which a project is assessed by a jury after several weeks of work. In this case, we can speak of a very product-oriented weighting, since in the end 'only' the final design, the result depicted on a presentation drawing, is evaluated.

In contrast, process-oriented work can focus on the first steps of the task from the moment an exercise is assigned. Students sketch, design and build models at various

Arbeitsweise „Produktorientiert"
'Product-oriented' approach

Arbeitsweise „Prozessorientiert"
'Process-oriented' approach

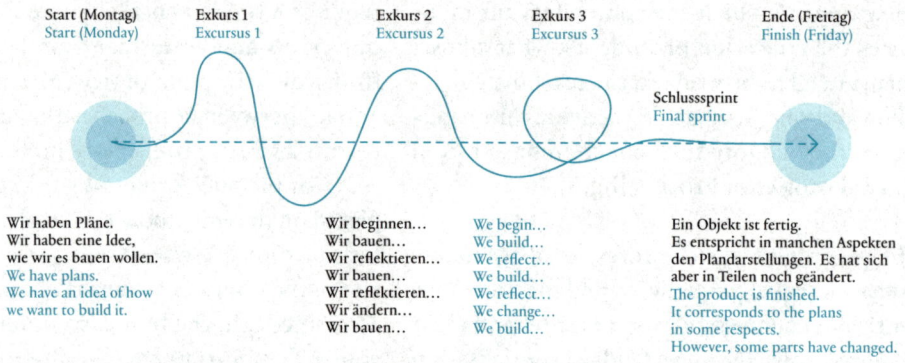

2   Während bei der produktorientierten Arbeitsweise ein sehr geradliniger Arbeitsprozess verfolgt wird, können sich bei der prozessorientierten Herangehensweise noch wesentliche Änderungen am Projekt ergeben. While the product-oriented working method follows a very straightforward work process, the process-oriented approach can still result in significant changes to the project.

scales, they develop prototypes and thus have the freedom to pursue a wide range of ideas through to the completion of the project. A key difference from the product-oriented approach is that all these intermediate steps later also form an integral part of the work presented. However, the products created as part of the design process, such as sketches, models and full-scale prototypes, must be carefully selected and documented so that they can later be presented as part of the larger story, the process.

This combination of preparing a design basis and then actually implementing it through manual work has its roots in the curriculum of the architecture programme at the University of Antwerp. As part of the one-semester course 'Spatial Tectonics; Studio Architectonisch Ontwerp 1:1', students were given the task of designing and building wooden furniture under the guidance of Prof. Mario Rinke (UANTWERP), Leen De Brabandere (UANTWERP) und Alessandro Tellini (ETH Zurich). Over a four-week period, each group of students was assigned a space, either on the University of Antwerp campus or in one of the city's museums, for which they did analysis, developed potential design solutions and produced initial prototypes.

During the fifth week, these concepts were realised in final form as pieces of furniture. The benches, chairs and tables were then distributed to their designated locations in the city, where they were exhibited and evaluated in their intended surroundings. In addition to purely spatial criteria, this diverse collection of furniture pieces also had to meet other requirements. For example, all the pieces were made without any steel parts—without screws or nails whenever possible—and only from solid wood. The tools provided were also deliberately limited to chisels, a handsaw or (occasionally) a cordless drill. For the students, these specifications presented additional challenges in terms of the wood joinery and the processing steps required. in terms of the wood joints that could be made and the steps involved in carrying out the work.

On the basis of these observations and numerous discussions, we can retrospectively make a weighted assessment of the respective working methods according to their product-oriented or process-oriented focus. From this perspective, working groups with a more product-oriented strategy settled on their designs very early on. In most cases, a solution was chosen that could be implemented with a reasonable amount of effort and a correspondingly predictable risk [fig. 2].

In this comparison, the more process-oriented teams also had designs and plans for building their pieces ready at the start of the 1:1-scale week. The design and geometry of some of these pieces of furniture were more expressive and therefore potentially more complex to build. While the projects of the process-oriented groups may have started on a similar, well-grounded basis at the beginning of the week (plans, mock-ups, models), the actual complexity of the form only became apparent as the construction work progressed. Some general observations can also be drawn from this discussion of the two different approaches.

- *Stability and self-explanatory use:* The finished objects are ultimately intended to provide seating for museum visitors. Once in place, the objects must be self-explanatory and work well for a variety of people. Appropriate functionality, stability and safety of use must be guaranteed.

Im Rahmen der fünften Woche wurden diese Konzepte final als Möbelstücke umgesetzt. Die Bänke, Stühle und Tische wurden abschliessend an die jeweiligen Orte in der Stadt verteilt und somit in der projektierten Umgebung ausgestellt und bewertet. Diese zum Teil sehr unterschiedlichen Möbel hatten neben räumlichen Kriterien noch weitere Vorgaben zu erfüllen. So wurden alle Objekte ohne Stahlteile, möglichst ohne Schrauben oder Nägel und lediglich aus massivem Holz hergestellt. Die dafür bereitgestellten Werkzeuge wurden ebenfalls bewusst auf Stemmeisen, eine Handsäge oder (manchmal) einen Akkubohrer reduziert. Für die Studierenden brachten diese Vorgaben weitere Herausforderungen in Bezug auf die Holzverbindungen und die dabei notwendigen Bearbeitungsschritte.

Aufbauend auf diesen Beobachtungen sowie zahlreiche Gespräche kann retrospektiv eine Gewichtung der jeweiligen Arbeitsweisen zwischen produkt- oder prozessorientiertem Fokus diskutiert werden. So gesehen haben Arbeitsgruppen mit einer produktorientierten Strategie ihr Design bereits sehr früh fixiert. In den meisten Fällen wurde dabei eine Lösung gewählt, die mit angemessenem Aufwand und entsprechend kalkulierbarem Risiko umgesetzt werden konnte [Abb. 2].

Im Vergleich dazu hatten auch die prozessorientierteren Arbeitsgruppen zu Beginn der 1:1-Woche ein Design sowie einen Plan für das zu fertigende Objekt bereitliegen. Die Gestaltung und Geometrie der Möbelstücke waren zum Teil expressiver und somit in der Umsetzung unter Umständen aufwendiger. Obwohl die Projekte der prozessorientierten Gruppen zu Beginn der Woche möglicherweise auf einer ähnlichen, gut fundierten Basis begonnen hatten (Pläne, Mockups, Modelle), zeigte sich erst in der fortschreitenden Umsetzung die tatsächliche Komplexität der Form. Aus dieser Diskussion über die produkt- oder prozessorientierte Herangehensweise können zudem noch übergeordnete Beobachtungen zusammengetragen werden.

- *Standsicherheit und selbsterklärende Nutzung*: Die fertigen Objekte sollen am Ende für Besuchende von Museen eine Sitzmöglichkeit bieten. Aufgestellt müssen die Objekte also für eine Vielzahl an Menschen funktionieren und entsprechend selbsterklärend ausgelegt sein. Eine entsprechende Nutzungssicherheit, Funktionalität und Standsicherheit muss gewährleistet werden.
- *Gestalterisch repräsentativ*: Die Objekte werden im öffentlichen Raum ausgestellt und sollen eine entsprechende Qualität hinsichtlich der Gestaltung und Umsetzung aufweisen. Ein geradliniger Hocker ist somit einfacher, wobei eine unpraktische Sitzskulptur möglicherweise auch noch als unpassend wahrgenommen werden kann. Als Studierendenprojekte repräsentieren sie zudem die Universität im öffentlichen Raum.
- *Handwerkliche Umsetzbarkeit*: Die Objekte werden in letzter Konsequenz von den Planenden eigenhändig hergestellt. Ihr Design sollte somit entsprechend innovativ und anspruchsvoll sein, jedoch muss die Form auch mit der vorhandenen Infrastruktur und den handwerklichen Fähigkeiten der Gruppe umsetzbar sein. Ein zu einfaches Design könnte am Ende langweilig wirken, wohingegen ein zu extrovertiertes Projekt unter Umständen an der Umsetzung scheitert [Abb. 3].

3   Bearbeitungsschritte Möbelbauprozess während der „Maak Week" in Antwerpen, März 2024. Steps in the furniture-making process during the 'Maak Week' in Antwerp, March 2024.

- *Artistically representative:* The pieces will be exhibited in public spaces and should therefore be of an appropriate quality in terms of design and execution. A rectilinear stool is therefore simpler, whereas an impractical seating sculpture might also be perceived as inappropriate. As student projects, they are also representative of the university in the public realm.
- *Handicraft feasibility:* The pieces will ultimately be built by hand by the designers themselves. Their design should be innovative and ambitious, but the form must therefore also be buildable with the existing infrastructure and the group's manual skills. A design that is too simple could end up looking boring, while a project that is too extroverted may not be feasible under the circumstances [fig. 3].

All these requirements, some internal and some external, necessarily demand that the students meet correspondingly high standards. Risks associated with the production process or unplanned changes in the project can only be resolved to a limited extent during the weeklong execution, which makes the execution correspondingly risky. Based on our observations, we would therefore attribute a more product-oriented approach to the majority of the projects. Some of the clearer designs have easily built joinery details. The chosen size of a piece is also decided pragmatically, and the complexity of the handicraft involved is easily manageable. As a result of these logical and often rather pragmatically motivated strategies, some groups had already completed their piece of furniture on the second day of work.

While some groups had already completed their pieces, others only realised the full

All diese zum Teil internen, zum Teil externen Vorgaben bringen eine entsprechend hohe Vorgabe mit sich, die es zu erfüllen gilt. Risiken im Herstellungsprozess bzw. ungeplante Änderungen im Projekt können in der Umsetzungswoche nur noch bedingt gelöst werden, was eine Umsetzung entsprechend riskant macht. Aus unseren Beobachtungen würden wir somit einem Grossteil der Projekte eine eher produktorientierte Herangehensweise zuschreiben. Die zum Teil klaren Designs haben umsetzbare Verbindungsdetails. Ebenso ist die gewählte Grösse eines Objektes pragmatisch entschieden und die Komplexität der handwerklichen Herstellung gut bewältigbar. Bedingt durch diese logischen und zum Teil eher pragmatisch motivierten Ansätze ergab es sich, dass manche Gruppen bereits am zweiten Arbeitstag mit ihrem Objekt fertig wurden.

Während manche Gruppen also bereits ihre Objekte fertig umgesetzt hatten, eröffnete sich bei anderen erst am zweiten und dritten Tag die volle Tiefe der Herstellung. So waren zum Teil die sehr komplexen Knotenpunkte (schräge Winkel, runde Fügungen) oder auch die immense Anzahl der Verbindungen (+100 Knotenverbindungen) grosse Herausforderungen, die es zu bewältigen galt. Bedingt durch das doch sehr knapp vorgegebene Zeitfenster von fünf Tagen für die Umsetzung wurden die gestalterischen Entscheidungen mit fortlaufender Zeit zugunsten umsetzbarer Lösungen getroffen. Komplexe Knoten wurden vereinfacht, Verbindungen letztlich mit anderen Lösungen umgesetzt, um das Ziel, ein Möbelstück fertigzustellen, nicht in Gefahr zu bringen. Aus einer beobachtenden Perspektive waren dabei gerade diese finalen Schritte in Bezug auf die Lernkurve der Studierenden sicherlich als bemerkenswert zu beurteilen. Während andere Gruppen bereits den dritten Tag auf einer fertigen Bank verbrachten hatten, mussten hier noch in letzter Minute pragmatische Lösungen erarbeitet und umgesetzt werden.

Aus einer übergeordneten didaktischen Perspektive darf dabei die wesentliche Frage gestellt werden, welche Strategie, welche Form des Arbeitens und Lernens in zukünftigen Lehrformaten eine Gewichtung zugeschrieben werden soll. Es stellt sich die Frage, wie ein entsprechender Unterricht ausgeformt werden muss und letztlich eine adäquate Beurteilung gewährleistet werden kann. Ist es das Ziel einer Lehrveranstaltung, dass Studierende klare Arbeitspläne, umsetzbare Entwürfe und sichere Ergebnisse abliefern? Oder sollen progressive Ideen, möglicherweise die Grenzen der eigenen handwerklichen Fähigkeiten und ein entsprechendes Risiko im final präsentierten Objekt verfolgt werden?

Grundlegend kann gesagt werden: Je zahlreicher die zu erreichenden Vorgaben sind (Robustheit, Herstellung, Funktion, Gestaltung, Budget, Material etc.), desto mehr wird eine Vielfalt der individuellen Lösungsvorschläge eingeschränkt. Ein öffentlicher Einsatz der Objekte bedeutet eine entsprechende Sichtbarkeit der Objekte, jedoch auch notwendige Sicherheits- und Nutzbarkeitsanforderungen. Eine Vorgabe bei der Materialwahl bringt eine gestalterische Einheitlichkeit der Objekte, jedoch auch eine formelle Begradigung der Vielfalt. 1:1-Projekte im Architekturstudium bringen für Studierende die Herausforderung einer zweigleisigen Herangehensweise zwischen Gestaltung, aber auch Umsetzung. Diese Erfahrungen schaffen wohl ein starkes Bewusstsein für spätere Planungs- und Umsetzungsprozesse an Bauprojekten.

depth of what needed to be done on the second and third days. In some cases, very complex junctions (skewed angles, rounded joints) or the sheer number of connections (over 100 joints) were major challenges to overcome. Due to the very tight time frame of 5 days for implementation, design decisions were increasingly made in favour of feasible solutions as time progressed. Complex joints were simplified, and connections were ultimately made using other methods so as not to jeopardise the goal of completing a piece of furniture. From an observer's perspective, these final steps in particular were certainly remarkable when considering the students' learning curve. While some groups already spent the third day sitting on a finished bench, others were forced to find and implement pragmatic solutions at the last minute.

From a broader didactic perspective, the key question is which strategy — which way of working and learning — should be prioritised in future teaching formats. And there is the question of how to devise appropriate teaching activities and, ultimately, how to ensure appropriate assessment. Is the aim of a course to ensure that students produce clear work plans, feasible designs and reliable results, or should more innovative ideas be encouraged in the pursuit of a final product that may push the limits of the students' own manual skills, with the risks that this entails?

As a general rule, the more requirements that need to be met (robustness, production, function, design, budget, material, etc.), the more limited the variety of individual solutions. Public use of the finished pieces means they will have visibility, but it also imposes necessary requirements for safety and usability. Specifying the material to be used brings uniformity to the design of the pieces but also levels out the formal diversity. By incorporating full-scale projects into the architecture programme, students are confronted with the challenge of a dual approach that bridges design and execution. This experience is likely to create a stronger awareness for later planning and implementation processes in building projects.

In principle, it is not possible or even necessary to draw a sharp line between process- and product-oriented working methods. As it turned out, some of the creations were barely able to support their own weight, let alone the weight of people sitting on them. This was a less than favourable observation when evaluating the final object. However, if the focus of the project week is put on the actual learning curve and the experience gained by the students, then the results of some of the crooked objects are all the more impressive. While some of the projects met the requirements for seating furniture on the first day due to their simple and straightforward geometry, it was impressive to see how other groups developed solutions to problems that arose just before the presentation deadline.

However, a comparison of the Ebaholz project at the University of Liechtenstein with the project week in Antwerp reveals that the diversity and variability in the design of 1:1 studios is significantly more complex. While the students working on the Ebaholz project had an entire semester to conceive and develop their designs, the design-build project at the University of Antwerp was largely completed in the first 2–3 weeks. For the students in Antwerp, the manual execution of the work in the final week was a key experience criterion. In contrast, the components for the Ebaholz project were ultimately built by skilled contractors

Grundsätzlich ist es nicht möglich oder gar notwendig, eine scharfe Linie zwischen prozess- oder produktorientierten Arbeitsweisen zu ziehen. Wie sich zeigte, waren manche Sitzmöbel kaum imstande, ihr eigenes Gewicht, geschweige denn das von Besuchenden zu tragen. Für das finale, bewertete Objekt eine wenig erfreuliche Beobachtung. Wird der Fokus der Arbeitswoche jedoch auf die eigentliche Lernkurve, die gemachten Erfahrungen der Studierenden gelegt, ist es umso beeindruckender, welche Ergebnisse so manch krummes Objekt mit sich brachte. Während die einen Projekte anhand einer einfachen und überschaubaren Geometrie bereits am ersten Tag die Anforderungen eines Sitzmöbels erfüllten, war es beeindruckend, wie manche Gruppen noch kurz vor der Präsentation Lösungen für auftretende Probleme entwickelten.

Dass Vielfalt und Varianz in der Auslegung von 1:1-Studios bei genauer Beobachtung jedoch wesentlich komplexer sind, lässt sich bei einer Gegenüberstellung des Ebaholz-Projekts an der Universität Liechtenstein und der Projektwoche in Antwerpen aufzeigen. Während die Studierenden am Ebaholz-Projekt ein komplettes Semester für die Ausarbeitung des Entwurfes zur Verfügung hatten, wurde dieser Prozess an der Universität in Antwerpen bereits in den ersten zwei bis drei Wochen zu einem grossen Teil abgeleistet. Für die Studierenden in Antwerpen wurde dabei gerade die eigenhändige handwerkliche Umsetzung in der finalen Woche ein wesentliches Erfahrungskriterium. Im Gegensatz dazu wurden die Bauteile am Ebaholz-Projekt (bedingt durch Umfang, Aufwand und Robustheit) letztlich von Handwerksbetrieben umgesetzt. Wenngleich dieser Schritt zu Beginn ebenfalls durch Studierende angedacht gewesen war, setzte sich die Menge an benötigten Bauteilen und die Dauerhaftigkeit als einzuhaltende Randbedingung durch. Wie sich in der Betrachtung beider Projekte zeigte, müssen derartige Lehrveranstaltungen immer sehr projektbezogen und individuell ausgerichtet werden. Allerdings muss beachtet werden, dass aus allen Entwürfen nur eine Idee schliesslich im Gebäude umgesetzt werden konnte und diese Ausführung nicht durch die Studierenden selbst, sondern von Handwerkern durchgeführt wurde. Dadurch wird der Fokus deutlich auf den Prozess verlagert und birgt auch einen gewissen Konkurrenzkampf, der dem Format von Wettbewerben in der Architektur sehr ähnelt [Abb. 4].

Für die zukünftige Entwicklung von Lehrformaten bleibt also die Frage, worauf bei Lehrveranstaltungen eine Gewichtung gelegt werden soll, welche Lernziele definiert werden können und bis zu welchem Punkt diese Ergebnisse erreicht werden müssen. Nichtsdestotrotz muss gerade während der Ausbildung eine selbstständige Arbeitsweise durch prozessorientiertes Lernen, das auch Fehler, Änderungen und experimentelle Herangehensweisen zulässt, aufgebaut werden. Es liegt wohl in der Kernaufgabe einer Bildungseinrichtung, fortlaufend die produkt- oder prozessorientierten Arbeits- und Lehrmethoden zu reflektieren, um Absolventinnen und Absolventen bestmöglich auf spätere Herausforderungen vorbereiten zu können.

4 Vier Möbelstücke in ihrem Kontext, welche in der „Maak Week" in Antwerpen, März 2024 entstanden sind. Four pieces of furniture in their context, created during 'Maak Week' in Antwerp, March 2024.

(due to their size, complexity and the need for robustness). Although this last step was also originally intended to be carried out by the students, the number of components required and their durability became the critical conditions to be met. As observation of both projects has shown, such academic courses always have to be designed in a very project-specific and individual way. It should be noted, however, that of all the designs developed, only one idea could ultimately be implemented in the building, and that the actual work was carried out by skilled craftspeople, not by the students themselves. This clearly shifts the focus to the design process and also involves a certain degree of competition that is very similar to the format of architectural competitions [fig. 4].

Looking to the future development of teaching formats, there are still questions about what should be prioritised in courses, what can be defined as learning objectives and to what extent these outcomes must be achieved. Nevertheless, it is precisely during educational training that an independent way of working needs to be developed through process-oriented learning that allows for mistakes, changes and experimental approaches. It is arguably the core task of an educational institution to continually reflect on this matter of product- versus process-oriented working and teaching methods in order to best prepare graduates for their future challenges.

Ausgangssituation Initial situation

Prototypen Treppe
Prototypes Staircase

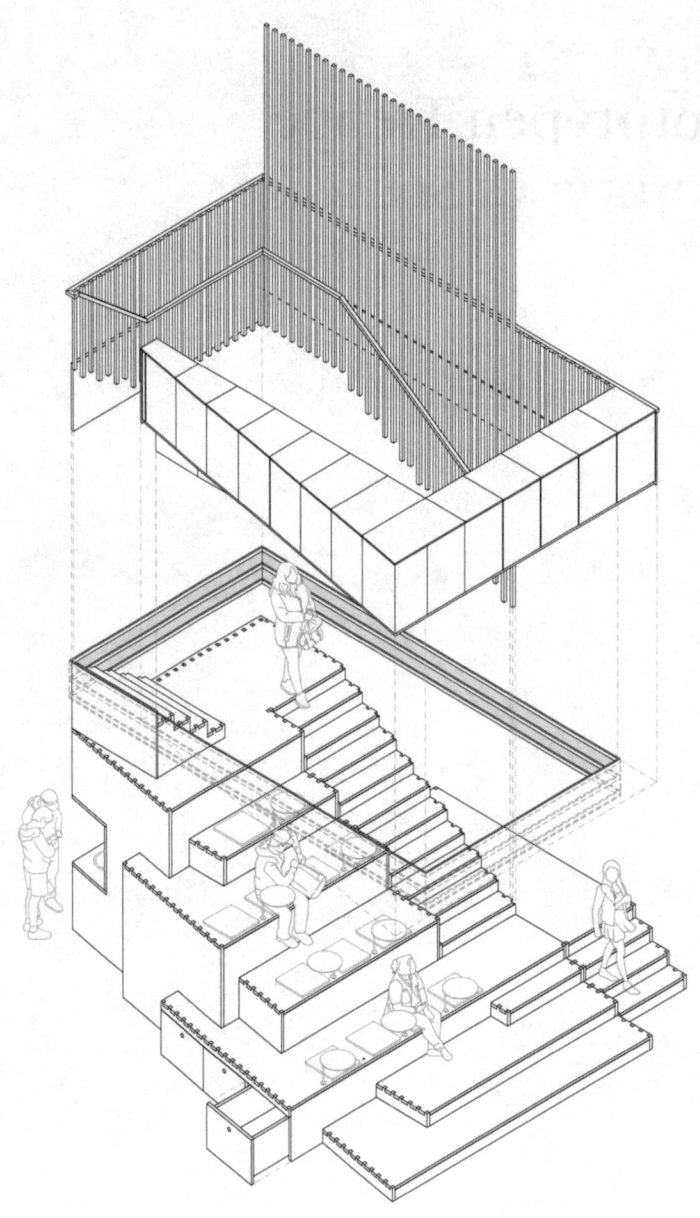

Magdalena Hagen, Kim Kosec, Asli Yavuz

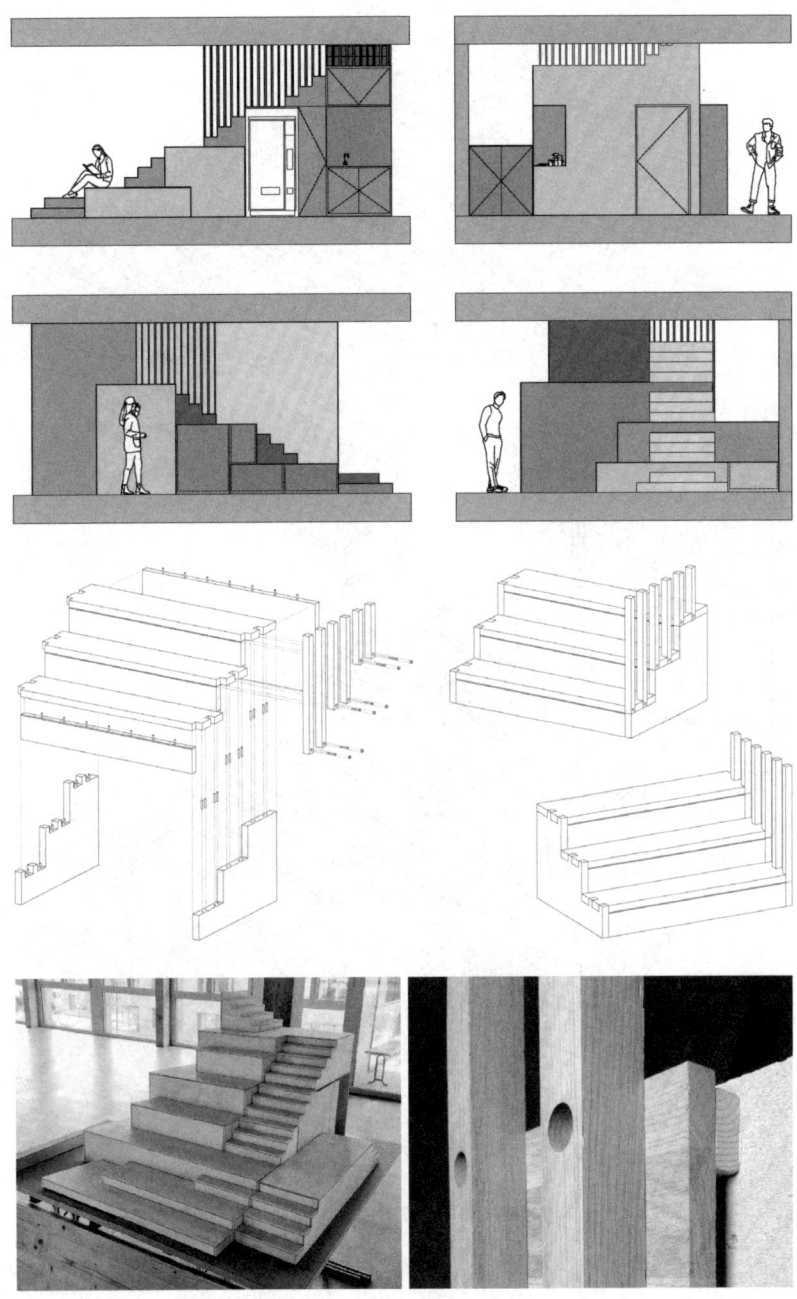

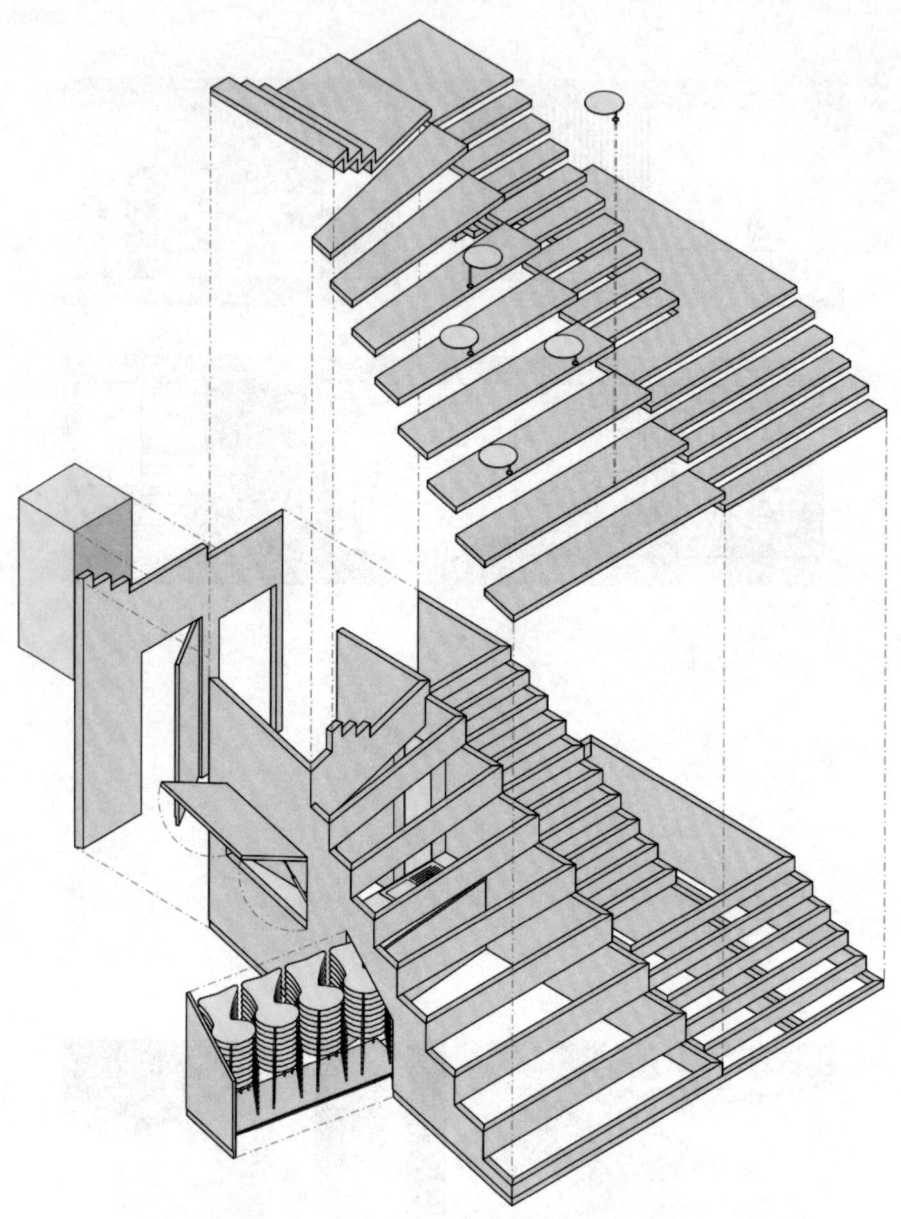

Franz-Felix Juen, Leon Reinprecht, Luca Strimmer

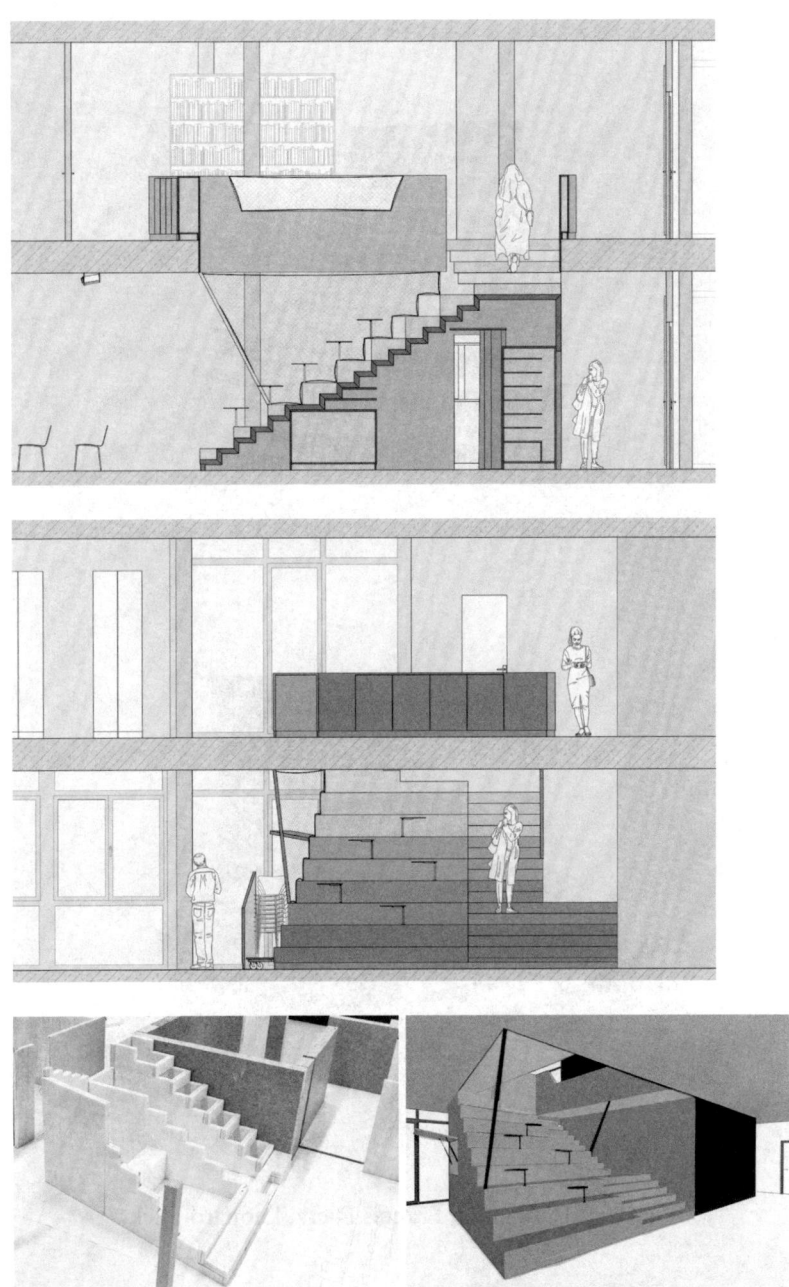

Pia Luisa Dablander, Francis Dietz, Leonard Flick

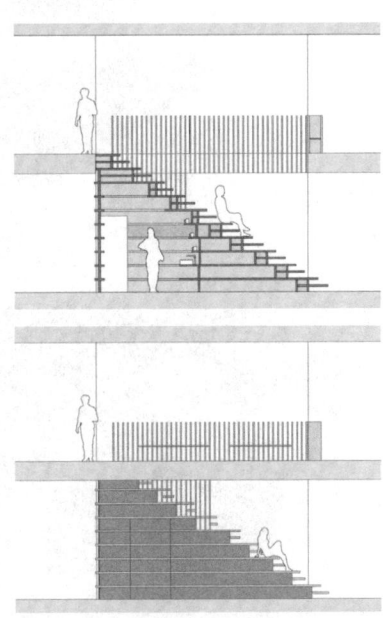

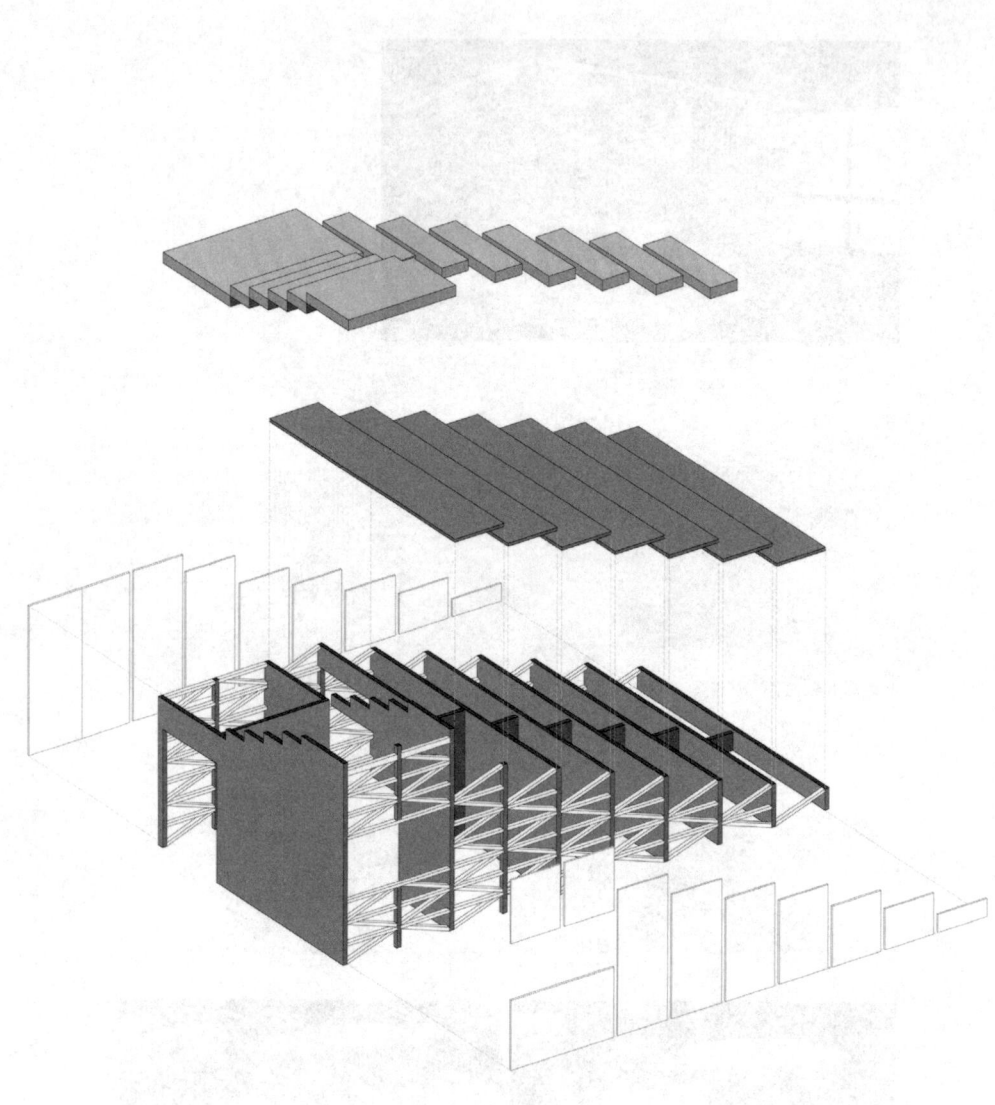

Selinay Ada, Rafaela Bertoni

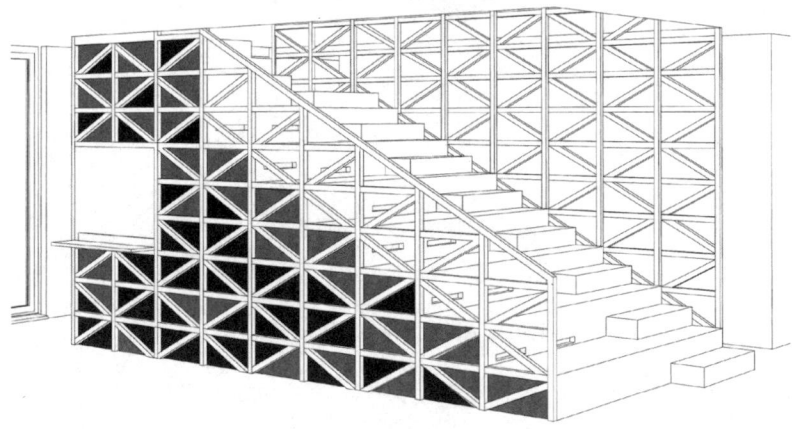

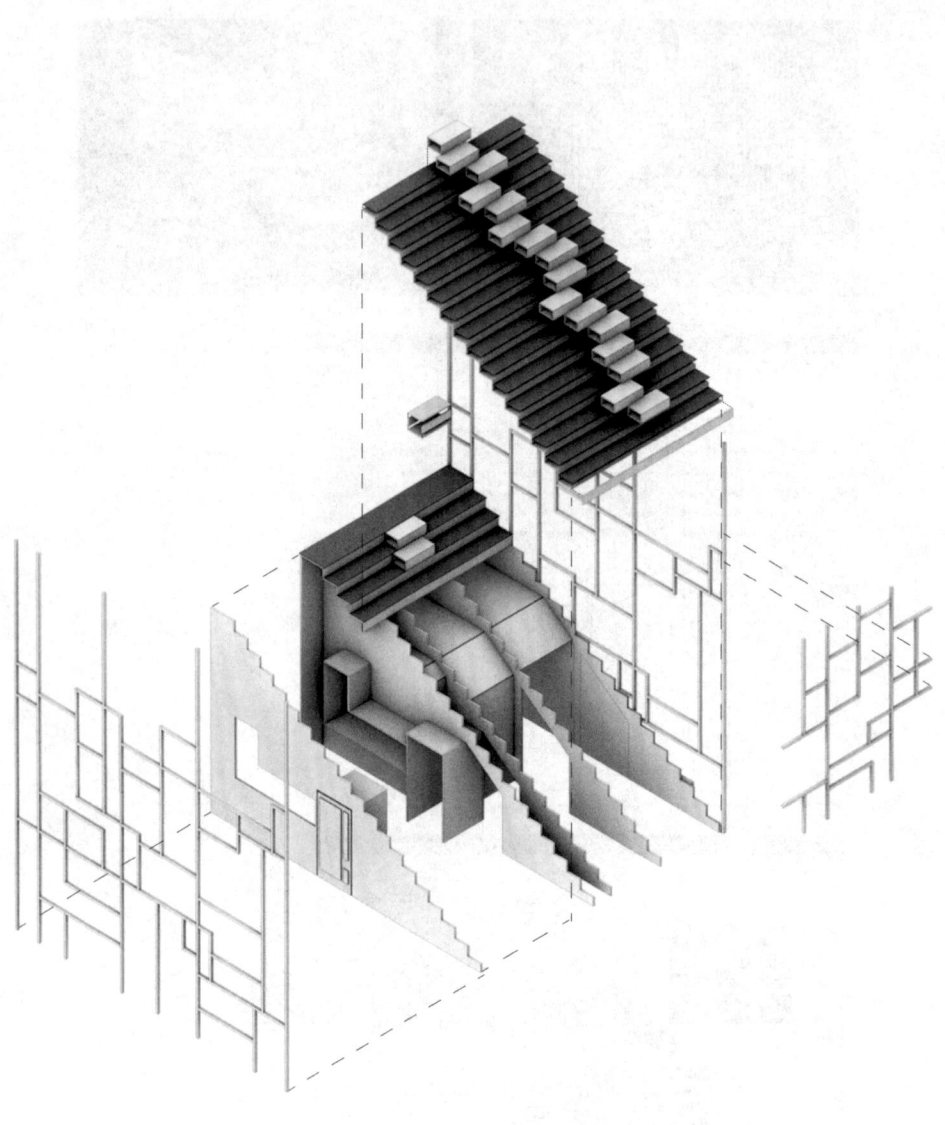

Laura Arroyave, Luis Mack

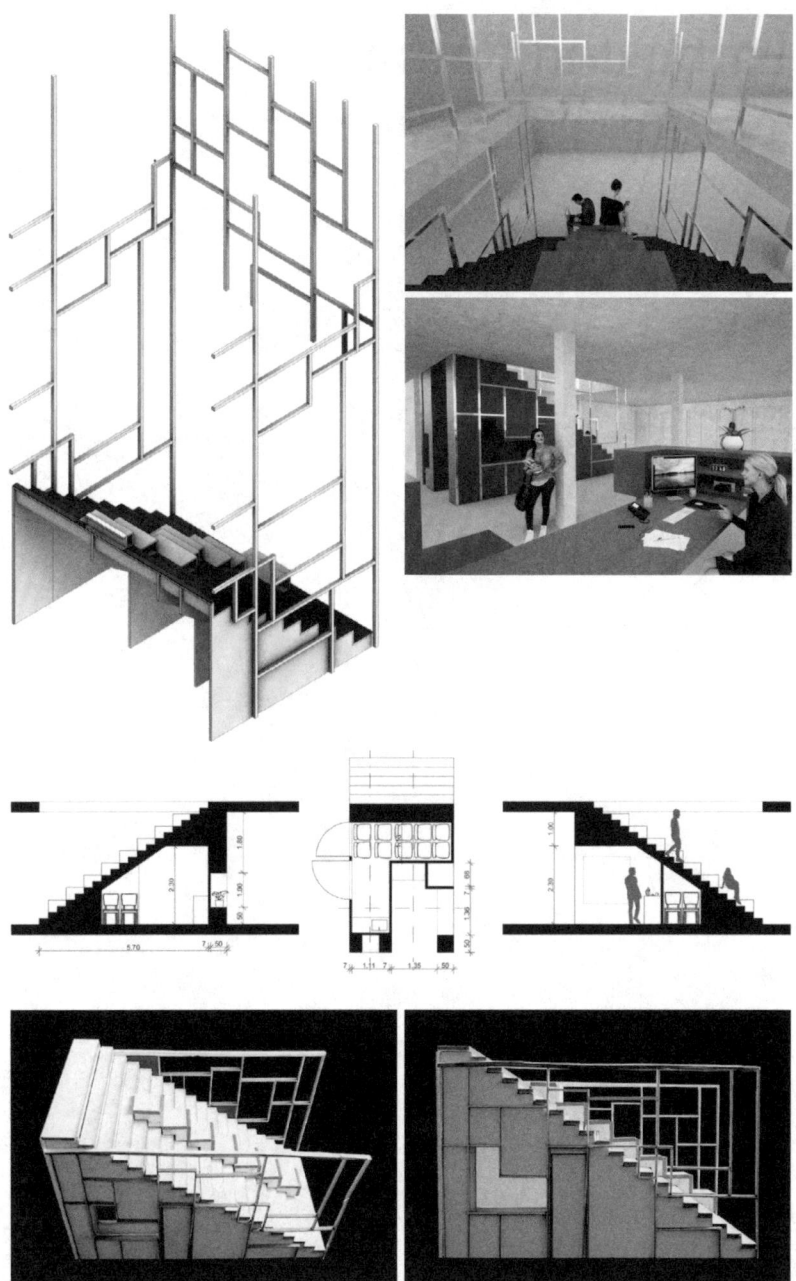

Farbe und Raum
Colour and Space

Marcella Wenger

Die digitalen Werkzeuge beiseite gelassen, stelle man sich Handskizzen vor, die mit Grafitstrichen und -schraffuren Ideen für Silhouetten architektonischer Hüllen offenbaren. Grundrisse, die Zellen und Zonen bilden, funktionale Ausnutzung mit sinnvollen Zugängen und Ausblicken waren im besten Fall für die Gestalt der ersten Skizze ausschlaggebend — wenn nicht, so ist die Raffinesse der ursprünglich gedachten Silhouette nur noch Erinnerung. Ein rudimentäres Modell kann einem Schnittmuster gleich ein Leitwerk für die weitere Ausgestaltung sein, doch das Konstrukt bleibt blutleer, solange das Schnittmuster ohne den Stoff gedacht ist.

Wenn Entwürfe von Couture oder Architektur auf Spielereien und Experimente mit sinnlichen, ästhetischen und funktionalen Eigenschaften von Material folgen, dann entsteht selbstverständlich Anmutendes — etwas, das aus sich selbst gewachsen scheint, somit autark und sogar als Solist in unterschiedlichen Kontexten kleiden und bestehen kann. Das Innenleben von so Gewachsenem, ob es nun hier ein Futteral als Kontrapunkt hat, da sachlich ausgestaltet oder gar nicht gefüttert ist — wenn es als Inneres, als Raum der Form gerecht wird, dann ist es dreidimensional in Licht und Schatten — stofflich und farbig erlebbar und gut.

Im Projekt „Farbstrategien in der Architektur" erforschen das Haus der Farbe und die Universität Edinburgh gemeinsam das raumgestalterische Potenzial von Farbe. Im Rahmen der Analyse von Bauten aus dem 20. und 21. Jahrhundert wurden Farben vor Ort referenziert und nachgemischt, um unterschiedliche Farbpaletten sichtbar zu machen und ausfindig gemachte Strategien zu veranschaulichen.

Nachhaltig beeindruckte nach dem Studium der Farben der Berliner Philharmonie und der Berliner Staatsbibliothek des Architekten Hans Scharoun (1893–1972) folgende Erkenntnis: Die Farben und ihre Modulierung, wie sie Scharoun in Aquarellen utopischer Architekturgebilde einsetzte, bilden körperhafte Atmosphären, die kongruent sind mit den tatsächlich gebauten. In beiden Bauten ist die Farbe untrennbarer Bestandteil der Architektur. Funktion und Nutzung, Konstruktion und Raumproportionen, Materialien und Oberflächenstrukturen, Licht und Schatten vereinen sich mit der Farbe zu einer Raumchoreografie. Farbe unterstützt dabei gestalterische Absichten und klärt Dimensionen, schafft Atmosphären und verfeinert die Raumwirkung, ohne eigenmächtig oder aufdringlich zu sein. Die sorgfältige farbliche Gestaltung jeder Einzelform berücksichtigt stets die Gesamtform. Die subtil gesteigerte Raumqualität ist intuitiv wahrnehmbar und lässt sich aber erst bei eingehender Beobachtung entschlüsseln. So stellt diese Strategie höchste Anforderungen sowohl an den architektonischen als auch farblichen Entwurf. Hans Scharoun, der offensichtlich mit allen sinnlichen Dimensionen, ganz besonders mit Materialfarben und Farbe, entworfen hat, suchte die Zusammenarbeit mit Lou Scheper-Berkenkamp (1901–1976), einer Farbgestalterin der ersten Stunde, um seine gestalterischen Intentionen präzise zu verwirklichen [Abb. 1, 2].

Wird der Aspekt der Farbgebung erst als finale Kür verstanden, dann stehen im besten Fall Funktion und Identität im Vordergrund — vor allem aber sind Entwurfsegos individuell getriggert und streben danach, mit Effekten, Originalität und angesagten Trends zu gefallen oder mit ikonischen Referenzen zu imponieren.

Einerseits unterliegen die Farbkollektionen von Beschichtungen, Textilien und

konfektionierten Funktionsoberflächen materialbedingten Möglichkeiten, haben oft den kommerzgesteuerten Mainstreamfilter passiert und sind limitiert. Fast zu viel gestalterische Freiheit andererseits liegt in den Anstrichstoffen. In systematischen Farbordnungen erscheint die Welt der Farben stimmig, übersichtlich und logisch aufgereiht wie die Tonfolge eines gut gestimmten Klaviers. Die Ordnungen erscheinen harmonisch und verleiten dazu, wie am Piano den „Flohwalzer" zu klimpern oder Tonleitern anzuschlagen. Farbverläufe aus Systemen und modische Kollektionen suggerieren Sicherheit. So steigern sich schliesslich beliebige Farbwerte, -kontraste und -quantitäten zu atmosphärischen Störgeräuschen im Gebauten, statt dass sich Raumproportionen, Materialien und Oberflächenstrukturen, Licht und Schatten zu einem Ganzen vereinen.

Experiment im Studium

In einem Experiment werden die Studierenden aufgefordert, unter Zeitdruck aus einer chaotischen Menge von 5500 verschiedenen, handgemischten Farbkarten einen Fünffarbenklang frei zu komponieren, der ihr individuelles farbgestalterisches Können repräsentieren soll — der Farbklang an sich soll umwerfend schön sein —, was etwa dem Druck entspricht, dem gestalterisch Tätige, seien es Floristinnen, Designerinnen oder Architektinnen, letztlich immer ausgesetzt sind. Die Stimmung im Atelier ist geschäftig, individuell fokussiert und angespannt. Vereinzelt tauchen Fragen auf, ob es sich um ein Interieur handelt oder was auch immer — die Antwort, Farbe per se, macht es nicht einfacher; Begriffe wie „Harmonie" oder „passen" und auch „Geschmackssache" sind zu hören. Am Ende des Zeitfensters sind die

1, 2   Aquarelle, Hans Scharoun, 1939–1945. Vom Ausbruch des Krieges an bis zur Kapitulation entstanden Tag für Tag Zeichnungen, Aquarelle, Entwürfe. Sie entstanden aus Selbsterhaltungstrieb und auch aus dem Zwange, sich mit der Frage nach der kommenden Gestalt auseinanderzusetzen. Quelle: „Hans Scharoun", Ausstellungskatalog, Akademie der Künste, Berlin 1967. *Watercolours, Hans Scharoun, 1939–1945. From the outbreak of the Second World War until the German surrender, Scharoun produced drawings, watercolours and sketches on a daily basis. Their creation was both a survival tactic and a means of addressing pressing questions around shaping the future. Source: Hans Scharoun, exhibition catalogue, Akademie der Künste, Berlin 1967.*

Farbe und Raum

Setting aside digital tools, imagine hand-drawn sketches that use graphite strokes and hatching to reveal concepts for the silhouettes of architectural forms. Floor plans that form cells and zones, maximising the functional use of space, creating sensible entry points and views to the outside were at best crucial to the configuration of the first sketch — and if not, the finesse of the originally conceived silhouette is just a memory. A rudimentary model, like a tailor's pattern, can be a guide for further elaboration of a design, but the construct remains anaemic as long as that pattern is conceived without considering the fabric.

When designs for couture or architecture are based on playing and experimenting with the sensual, aesthetic and functional properties of their materials, the result is something that naturally makes an impression — something that seems to have an inherent logic and is therefore self-sufficient and can present itself fully as a soloist in a variety of contexts. The inner life of something that has developed in this way, whether it has an outer shell as a counterpoint, because it is soberly designed, or is not lined at all — if it does justice to the form as an interior, as a space, then it is three-dimensional in light and shadow — tangible and good in terms of both material and colour.

In the project 'Colour Strategies in Architecture', the Haus der Farbe in Zurich and the University of Edinburgh jointly researched the potential uses of colour in spatial design. As part of the analysis of 20th and 21st century buildings, colours were determined on site and then replicated in order to visually portray different colour palettes and illustrate the identified strategies they represent.

After studying the colours used for the Berliner Philharmonie and the Staatsbibliothek zu Berlin, both designed by architect Hans Scharoun (1893–1972), the following insight made a lasting impression: The colours and their modulation, as used by Scharoun in watercolour sketches of utopian architectural forms, evoke physical environments that are congruent with the structures as built. In both buildings, colour is an integral part of the architecture. Function and use, construction and spatial proportions, materials and surface textures, light and shadow. They all combine with colour to create a spatial choreography. Colour supports design intentions and clarifies dimensions, creates atmospheres and refines the spatial impact without being heavy-handed or intrusive. The carefully considered colour of each individual form always takes into account the overall form. The subtly enhanced spatial quality is intuitively perceptible but can only be deciphered on closer inspection. This strategy places the highest demands on both the architectural and the chromatic design. Hans Scharoun, who clearly considered all the sensory dimensions of design, especially the colours of materials and applied finishes, enlisted the services of Lou Scheper-Berkenkamp (1901–1976), one of the earliest colour designers, to ensure the precise realisation of his design intentions [figs. 1, 2].

If the aspect of colouration is understood as the final artistic choice, then function and identity are best when foregrounded — but design egos are above all individually triggered and strive to please with impact, originality and hip trends, or to impress with iconic references.

On the one hand, the range of colours available for coatings, textiles and custom-made functional surfaces are subject to the possibilities offered by the materials themselves and are

Farbklänge fixiert und auf der Rückseite als „schön" gekennzeichnet.

Die Aufgabe des zweiten Experimentteils liegt auf der Hand. Es gilt in gleicher Weise einen Farbklang zu komponieren, der schlecht oder gar hässlich ist. Die Stimmung verändert sich markant. Es wird gelacht, gespielt und Zeitdruck scheint nicht vorhanden zu sein. Das weitere Prozedere wiederholt sich. Die Farbklänge werden als hässlich gekennzeichnet.

Die Gegenüberstellung der beiden Gruppen ist aufschlussreich. Manchmal fragt man sich, ob der eine oder andere Farbklang nicht in die andere Gruppe gehört ... dazu später mehr. Das Kolorit aller „Schönen" wirkt insgesamt unbewegt, grau und gebrochen. Die „Schönen" in sich sind überwiegend monochrom, oft in Hell-Dunkel-Verläufen. Auch analoge Abstufungen sind vertreten, z. B. von kräftigem Gelb zu Rot. Die „Schönen" sind vertraut und eingängig.

Die Farbigkeit aller „Hässlichen" ist dagegen rhythmisch, kontrastreich und farbenfroh. Blasses Rosa, feuriges Pink, Zitronengelb, viele fast reine Farben kommen hier ins Spiel, meist aber in unkonventioneller Kombination mit Senf, Braun oder anderen Farben, die einzeln durchaus ambivalent konnotiert sein können. Viele der „Hässlichen" sind laut, fremd und reiben sich an unseren Sehgewohnheiten.

Fazit: Die Farbklänge, die unter dem Druck des Gefallens entstehen, sind gefällig, die einen elegant, die anderen rustikal, aber allen gemeinsam ist, dass sie leicht verständlich und kopierbar sind wie die Refrains atemloser Schlager, die, einmal gehört, zu Ohrwürmern mutieren. Je breiter das Gefallen, desto näher das Mittelmaß.

Nicht, dass die Kompositionen der zweiten Gruppe alle besser wären, aber das inspirierende Potenzial dieser Klänge liegt in der innovativen Kraft einzelner extravaganter Farbnachbarschaften und dem unerwarteten Zauber verboten geglaubter Kombinationen. Wenn wir uns also nicht von Konventionen einengen lassen, wenn wir das Unmögliche in Betracht ziehen, wenn wir wertfrei Wirkungen beobachten, dann sind wir in der Lage, nachhaltige Ästhetik zu schaffen – also Farbkompositionen zu entwickeln, die dem ersten Blick standhalten und jeden weiteren Blick mit Entdeckungen und Wirkungseffekten belohnen.

Farbästhetik im Prozess

Tektonische, material- und konstruktionstechnische Aspekte standen im Mittelpunkt des Entwurfsprozesses der einzelnen Elemente für den Rohbau des neuen Erweiterungsbaus der Universität. Da der Neubau bereits Wirklichkeit war, mussten die Studierenden ihre Ideen und Inspirationen transformieren, um die Anmutung der Material- und Farbkompositionen mit dem Kontext in einen sinnvollen Zusammenhang zu bringen.

So gestalteten die beiden Studentinnen Sara Lindner und Sara Stoll die Wände mit naturbelassenem, hellem Holz und Filz. Als Inspiration dienten ihnen ein Interieur aus einer Anwaltskanzlei in Bogotá, der Modulor von Le Corbusier und das plakative Rot aus der Corporate Identity der Universität – Zutaten, die für sich genommen vielversprechend sind, aber in ihrer Addition erst durch die sinnstiftende Transformation des Ganzen stimmungstragend werden konnten. Damit sich die Wandgestaltung so selbstverständlich in den Ort einfügt, dass eine sinnstiftende Identität entsteht, wurde die Farbpalette im Rahmen der verfügbaren Materialfarben und einer geschickten

often limited, having been filtered through the commercially controlled mainstream. On the other hand, there is almost too much creative freedom in the choice of coating materials. In systematic colour systems, the world of colour appears coherent, clear and logically arranged like the sequence of notes on a well-tuned piano. These systems appear harmonious and invite a simple response, like playing musical scales or 'chopsticks' on a piano. Predefined colour gradients and fashionable collections suggest reliability. Ultimately, in built works, a random array of hues, colour contrasts and quantities multiply to create ambient visual noise, rather than unifying the spatial proportions, materials, surface textures, light and shadow into a whole.

Studio experiment

In an experiment, architecture students at the University of Liechtenstein are asked to demonstrate their colour design skills by freely composing a five-colour combination from a chaotic collection of 5,500 different hand-mixed colour cards. They are given a short amount of time to make their choice, and it should be stunningly beautiful—which roughly corresponds to the pressure that creative professionals, be they florists, designers or architects, are regularly subjected to. The studio is buzzing with activity. The students are focused and tense. Occasionally there are questions about whether it's for an interior or whatever—and the answer, colour per se, doesn't make the task any easier. Things like 'harmony', 'match' and 'a matter of taste' can be heard. When the allotted time is up, the individual sheets of each colour combination are attached together and 'beautiful' is written on the back.

The second part of the experiment presents an obvious task: use the same method to compose a colour combination that is bad or even ugly. The mood changes dramatically. The students laugh and play, and the time pressure seemed to disappear. The rest of the procedure is repeated: each combination of five colours is labelled 'ugly'.

Comparing the two groups is an eye-opener. Sometimes you wonder if this or that colour combination should in the other category more on that later. The overall colouration of the 'beauties' seems static, grey and discontinuous. The 'beauties' themselves are predominantly monochrome, often in light-to-dark gradients. Analogous gradations, such as strong yellow to red, are also present. The 'beauties' are familiar and catchy.

The general colouration of all the 'uglies', on the other hand, is rhythmic, rich in contrast and full of vibrancy. Pale rose, fluorescent pink, lemon yellow; many almost-pure colours come into play here, but mostly in unconventional combinations with mustard yellow, brown or other colours that might have ambivalent connotations on their own. Many of the 'ugly' colour combinations are loud, unfamiliar and push us beyond our visual comfort zone.

Conclusion: The colour combinations that emerge when pressured to please are indeed pleasant—some are elegant, others rustic—but what they all have in common is that they are easy to understand and replicate, like the choruses of breathless pop songs that, once heard, morph into catchy tunes that get stuck in your head. The broader the appeal, the closer they come to mediocrity.

This is not to say that all the colour compositions in the second category are better, but the inspiring potential of these colour

mengenmässigen Verteilung der verschiedenen Farbwerte auf die Nutzung und die tektonischen Verhältnisse des Neubaus in Schaan abgestimmt. Die Arbeiten der Studierenden haben sich von Skizzen über Pläne, Diskussionen, Experimente, Prototypen, Scheitern und Weitermachen zur gebauten Realität entwickelt, sind dreidimensional in Licht und Schatten — stofflich und farblich im eklektischen Klangteppich des gesamten Hauses erlebbar.

combinations lies in the innovative power of unique, extravagant colour groupings and the unexpected magic of combinations thought to be forbidden.

The students at the University of Liechtenstein's Craft & Structure unit who carried out these experiments as part of the process of developing the walls, consequently learned that in order to create a lasting aesthetic when deciding on colours, they had to avoid the constraints of convention, consider the impossible and learn to observe effects with an open mind—in other words, they had to develop colour compositions that would stand up to a first glance but would also reward further observation with unexpected discoveries and impressionistic effects.

Colour aesthetics as part of the process

When designing the individual elements of the core and shell of the University's new annex, the designers were focused on aspects of tectonics, material properties and construction. The new building was already a reality, so the students had to adapt their ideas and inspirations to bring their material compositions and colour schemes into a meaningful relationship with the existing context.

For example, students Sara Lindner and Sara Stoll designed the walls using light-coloured untreated wood and felt. They were inspired by the interior of a lawyer's office in Bogotá, Le Corbusier's Modulor system, and the bold red colour of the University's corporate identity—ingredients that are promising in themselves, but which only achieve coherence when they are brought together by a meaningful transformation of the whole. To ensure that the wall design blends into its context in a sufficiently natural way to create a meaningful identity, the students adapted the colour palette to the functional and tectonic conditions of the new building in Schaan, working within the limits of the available material colours and skilfully distributing the various hues in careful proportions. The students' work evolved from sketches to plans and developed through discussion, experimentation, prototyping, failure and perseverance. It culminated in a built reality that is three-dimensional in light and shadow—and tangible in the eclectic tapestry of materials and colours throughout the building.

Konstruktions Details Construction details

Konstruktions Details Construction details

Prototypen Wand
Prototypes Wall

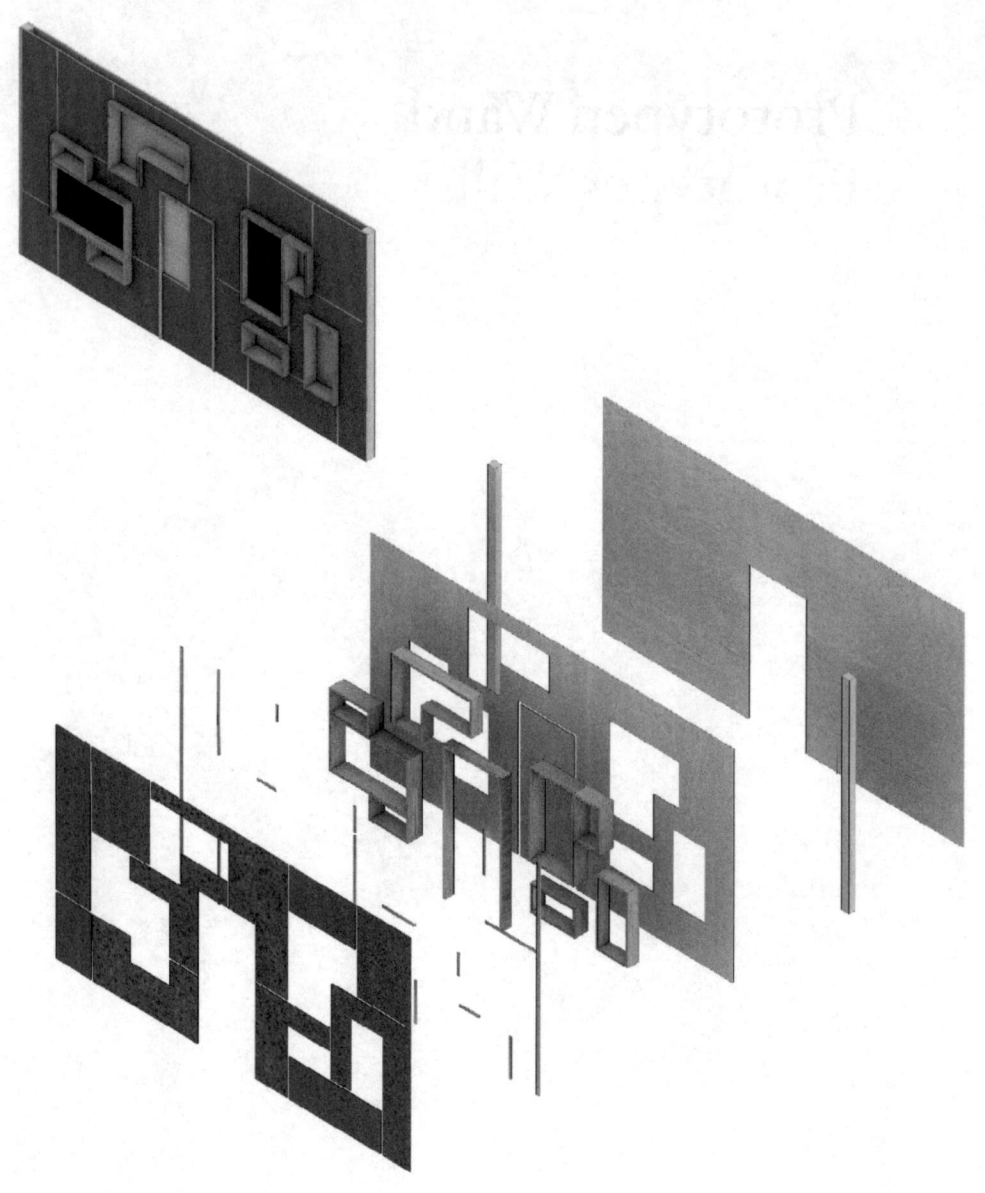

Selinay Ada, Laura Arroyave, Rafaela Bertoni, Luis Mack

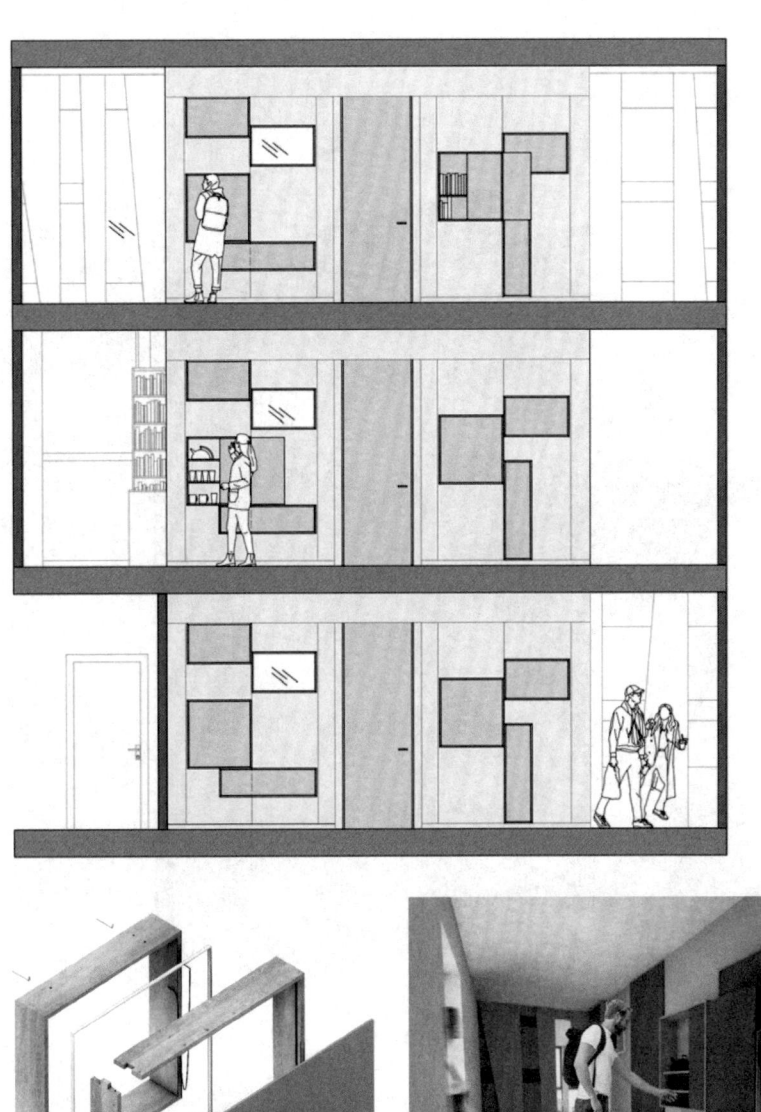

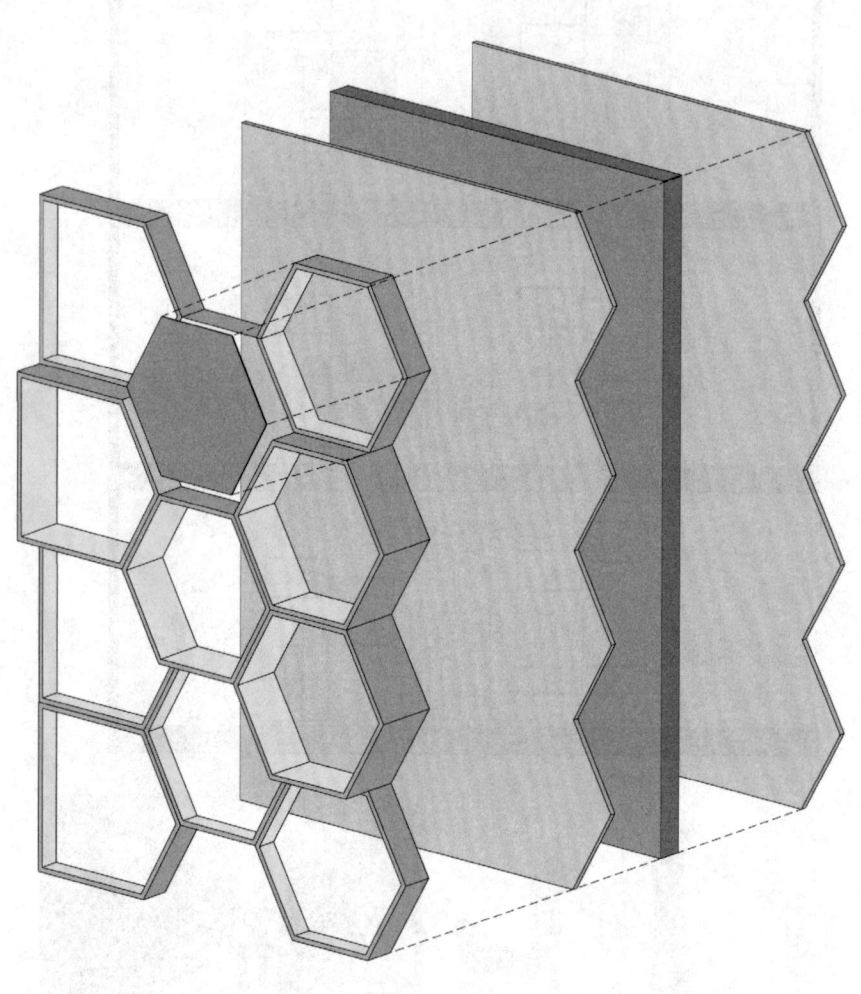

Rafaela Bertoni, Luca Strimmer

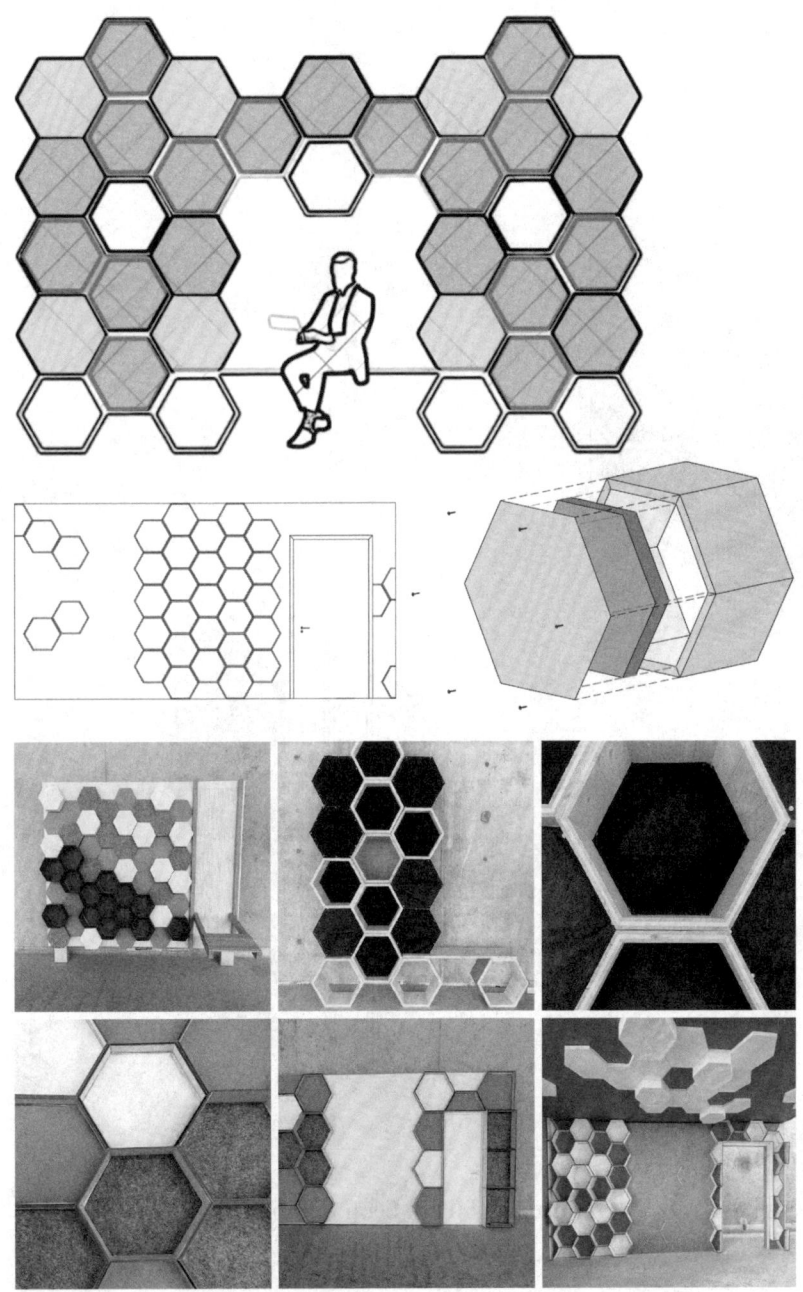

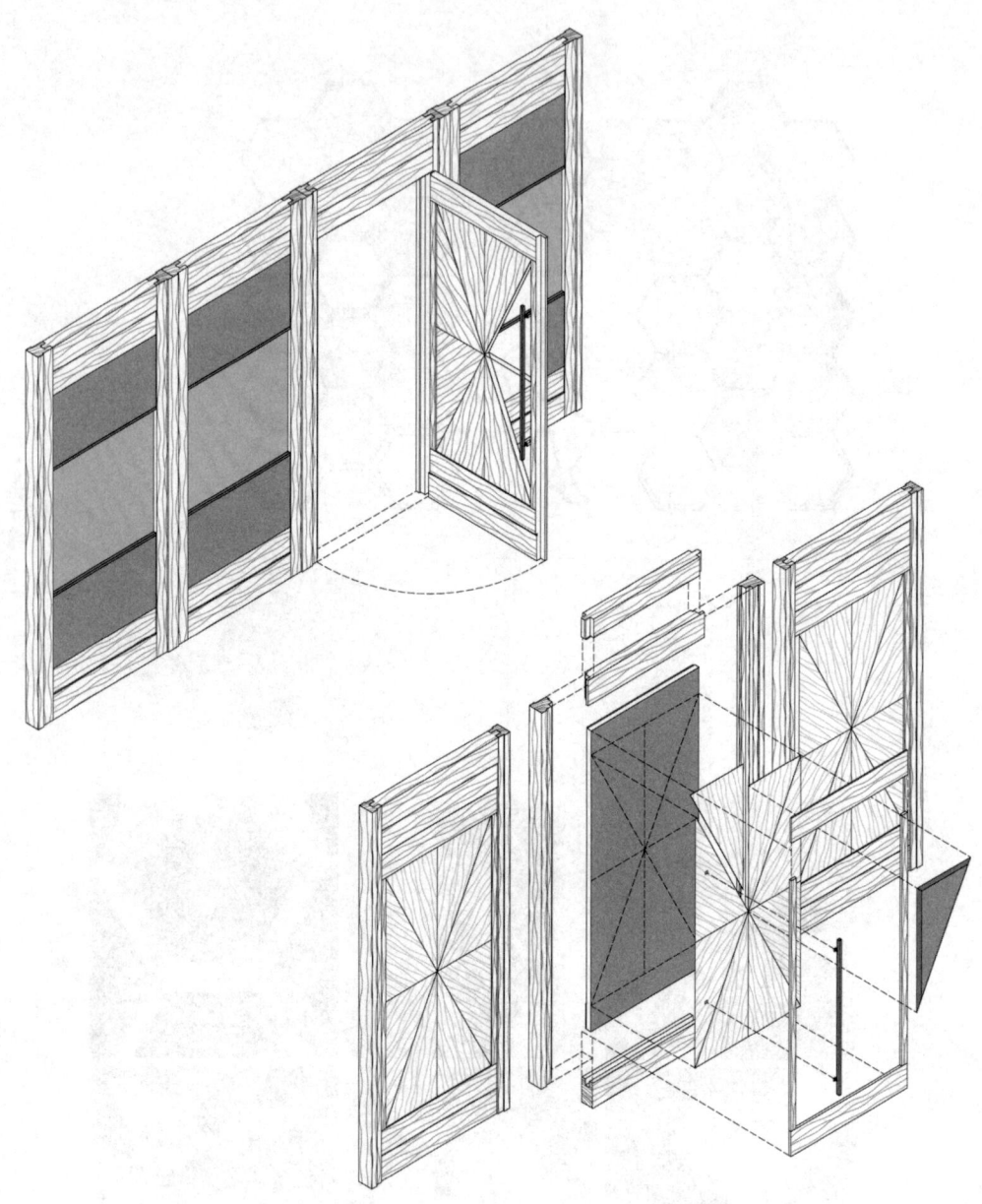

Franz-Felix Juen, Leon Reinprecht

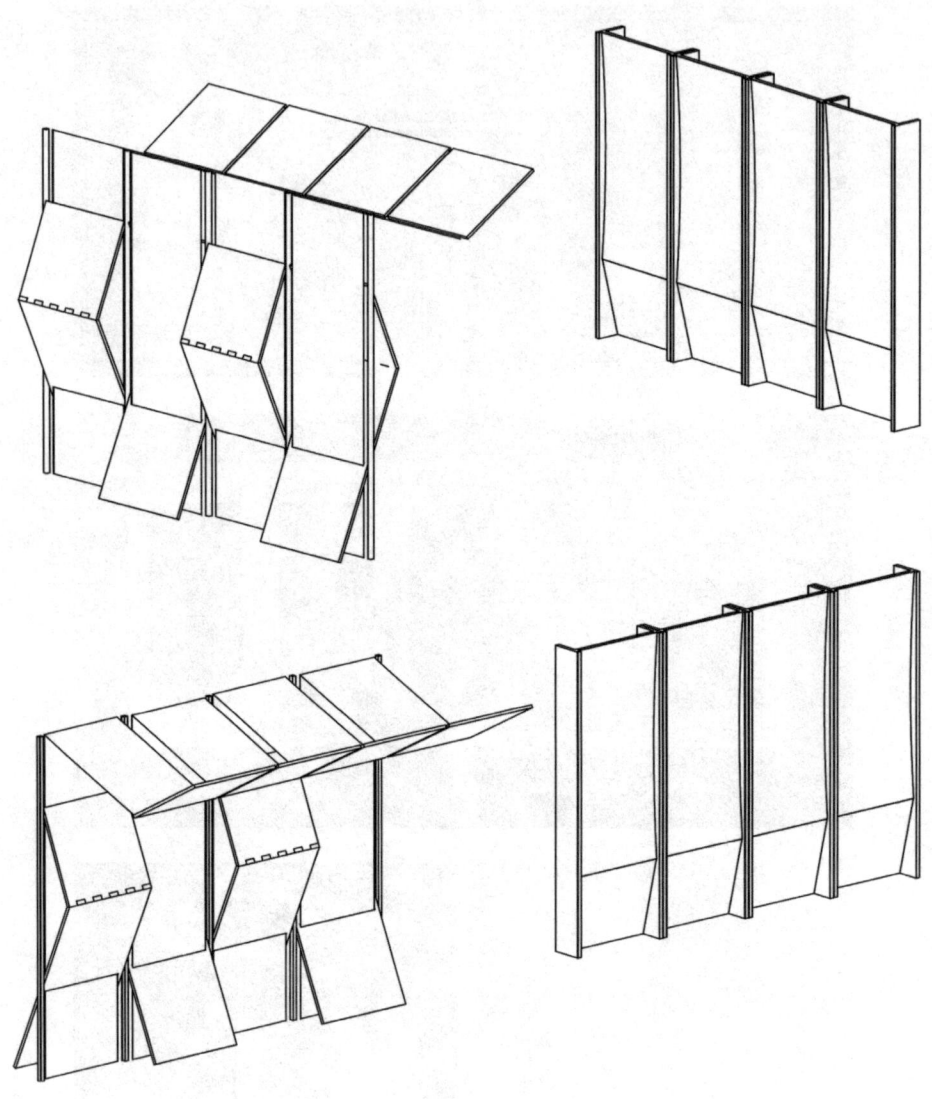

Magdalena Hagen, Kim Kosec, Asli Yavuz

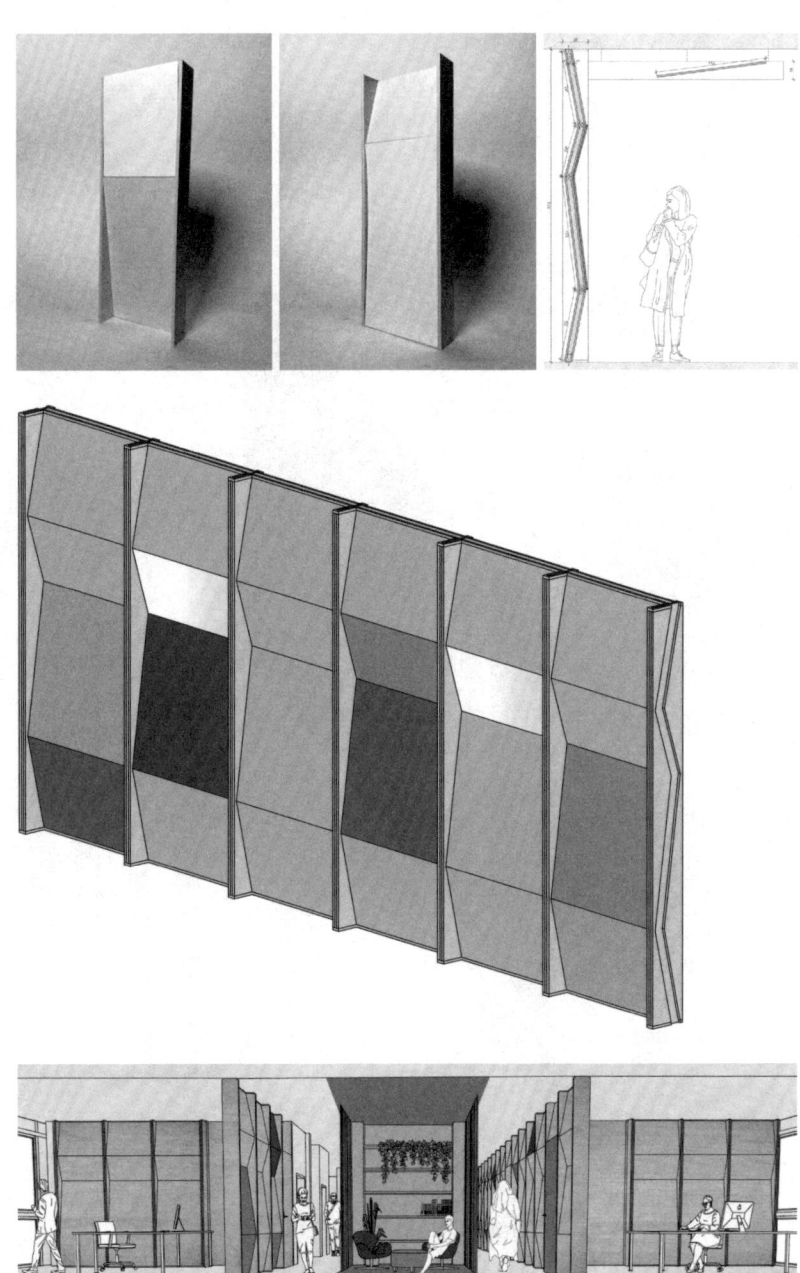

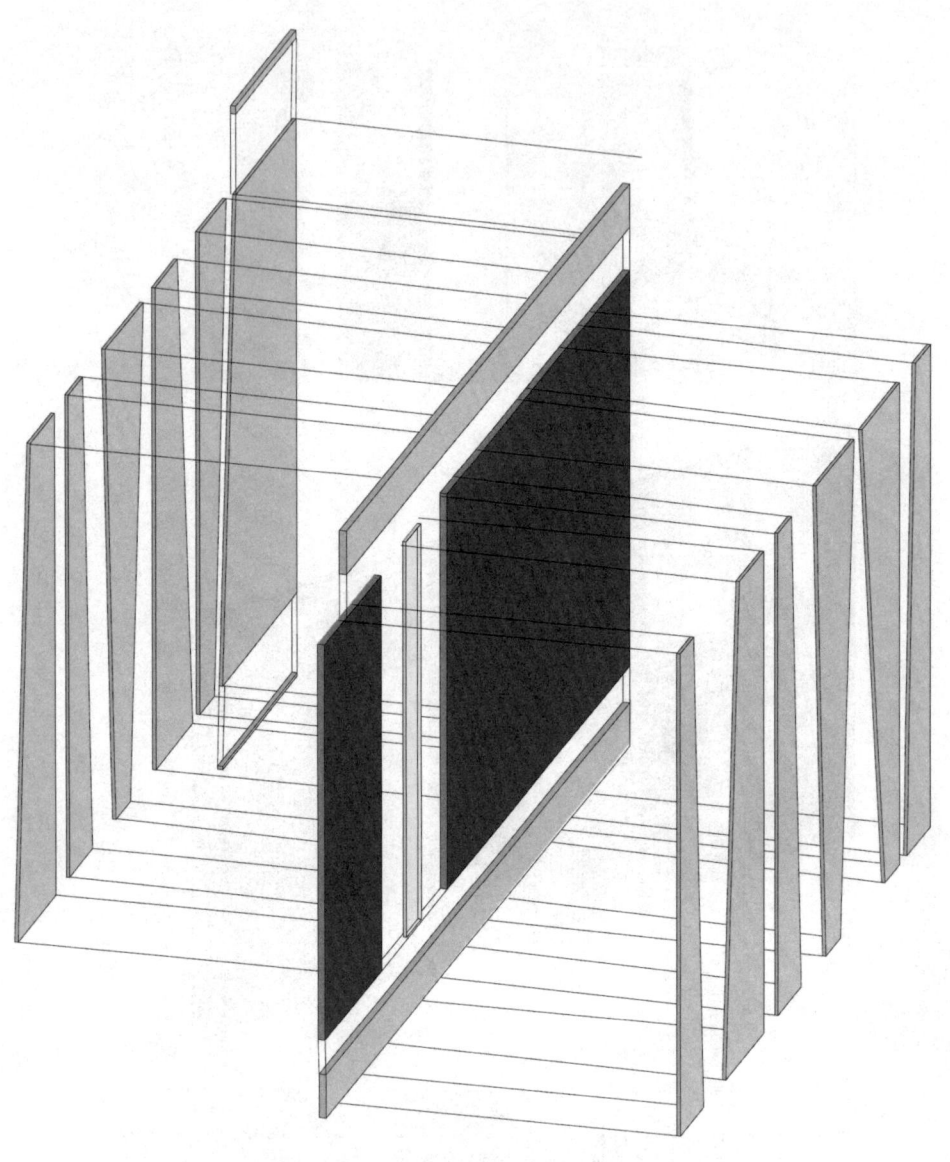

Sara Lindner, Sara Stoll

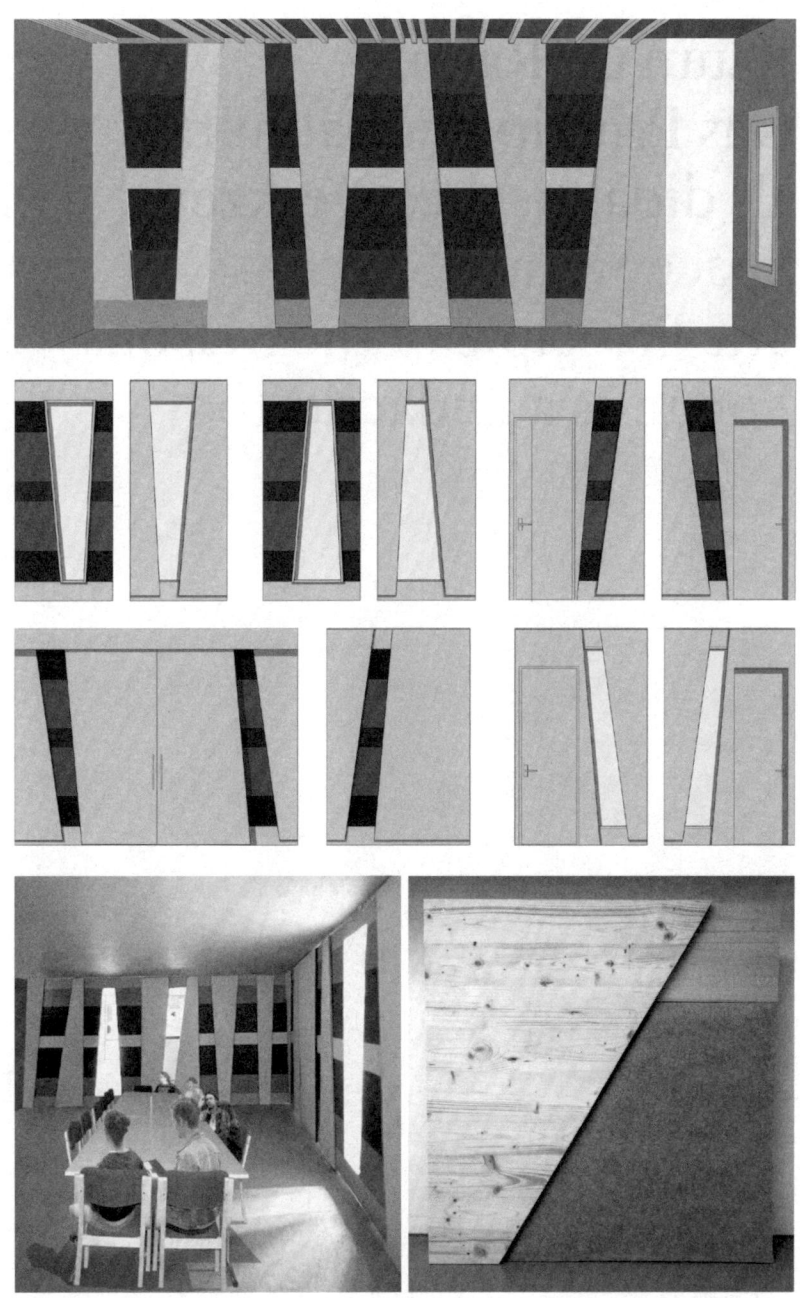

Raum im Raum —
Das Prinzip der Bauhütte als didaktisches Werkzeug

Space Within Space — The Principle of the Masons' Lodge as a Didactic Tool

Urs Meister
Carmen Rist-Stadelmann

Raum entsteht, wenn Grenzen gezogen und dreidimensional geklärt werden. Wände, Böden und Decken erlauben uns die Navigation im Raum und geben über die Taktilität ihrer Oberflächen Qualitäten und Atmosphären frei. Sie führen das Licht und den Schatten, reflektieren Farbtöne, sie definieren die Akustik und den Klang der Räume. Der holländische Architekt und Benediktinermönch Dom Hans van der Laan identifizierte drei Massstäbe in einem Gebäude: den „intimen Raum" oder „Arbeitsraum", den „begehbaren Raum", in dem Begegnungen stattfinden, und das „Sichtfeld", in dem das Gebäude in Beziehung zum Aussenraum tritt (Van der Lahn, 1989). Mit dieser Unterscheidung versuchten wir, das Projekt der Campus Extension zu ordnen und die innewohnenden Absichten konzeptionell zu klären. Wände, Raumteiler, Paravents, Gitterstrukturen und Hängewerke sollten als Elemente das neutrale innere Raumgeflecht gliedern.

Für Adolf Behne ist in der menschlichen Kultur das Praktische untrennbar mit dem Spieltrieb verbunden. „Er beweist seinen Spieltrieb auch an seinen Werkzeugen, die er über das streng Notwendige hinaus ebenmässig und schön formt, die er bemalt oder mit Ornamenten schmückt. Das Werkzeug ‚Haus' macht davon keine Ausnahme. Von Anfang an ist das Haus ebenso sehr Spielzeug wie Werkzeug." (Behne, 1926) Mit Holzbrettern, Stäben, Lamellen und weichen Materialien wie Filz, Stoffen oder Leder wurden die raumdefinierenden Elemente entsprechend ihrer Position mit Oberflächenpräsenz atmosphärisch aufgeladen und mit spielerischer Intuition gefügt [Abb. 1, 2].

Die Rolle der Wand

Mit Wänden schneiden wir also den Raum in abgezirkelte Einheiten, teilen ihn ein in Gefässe, die über Öffnungen miteinander kommunizieren. Das Wandelement wird zur Tür, zur Schiebewand, wird aufgeklappt, gefaltet, gedreht und öffnet oder schliesst Räume. Die Wände im Ebaholz zu bauen, erforderte ein System, das ein ganzes Set von Raumübergängen ermöglichen soll. Das System erlaubte es, Räume flexibel und entsprechend den Anforderungen der Benutzer zu gestalten und je nach Wunsch zu „verdichten und verdünnen", so wie es Gaston Bachelard in seiner „Poetik des Raumes" beschrieben hatte (Bachelard, 1960).

Spätestens seit die moderne Architektur vor über hundert Jahren proklamierte, dass die Wand als Raumbegrenzung von der tragenden Funktion gelöst werden sollte, wurde sie von einer statischen Aufgabe im Strukturgerippe des Bauwerks befreit und konnte sich auf ihre ureigene Rolle beschränken, die Räume zu definieren. Die Wand verhält sich seither wie eine Kulisse grundsätzlich im Hintergrund, um die Protagonisten des Raums — Treppen, Möbel und vor allem die Personen als Figuren im Raum — ihre Rolle im täglichen Drama spielen zu lassen. Doch unterschätzen wir nicht die Wand in ihrer eigenen Bedeutung als Trägerin nicht nur von räumlicher Information, sondern als materielle Erscheinung. Diese wurde in der Entschlackungskur des Funktionalismus vollkommen negiert, womit die Wand zu einer blassen Leinwand wurde, hell, flach und möglichst glatt.

Die Wand aber trägt seit jeher eine ganz andere Tiefe in sich, die schon im Wort angelegt ist. Das deutsche Wort Wand geht zurück auf Gewand und damit auf einen leichten,

textilen Abschluss, der eindeutig auf die Herkunft vom Zelt hindeutet. Sind die ersten Räume der Menschen nach den Höhlen und damit dem Erdbau zugeordneten Schwere später die Zelte der Nomaden, welche transportabel sein mussten, gleichzeitig falt- oder rollbar, in jedem Fall leicht. Damit kamen die primitiven textilen Herstellungstechniken gut zurecht, Gottfried Semper weist auf diesen Ursprung in „Der Stil" hin (Semper, 1860). Knüpf- und Webtechniken liessen nicht nur die Herstellung von Teppichen, sondern auch von Decken, Wandbehängen und gar Zäunen zu. So liessen sich Einfriedungen genauso errichten wie Zelte, Jurten und mobile Behausungen schlechthin [Abb. 3].

Das Kleid des Raums

Das Leichte, Weiche, Umhüllende bedurfte gleichzeitig des tragenden Skeletts, seien es die Scherengitter der Jurten oder die leichten Tragskelette der Zeltstangen. Eine frühe Vorwegnahme des in der Moderne proklamierten Auftrennens von Tragen und Trennen, was in der Konstruktionslogik des ephemeren Bauens natürlich entwickelt worden war. Im Weben, Knüpfen und Binden der leichten Wände und Gewände ist eine weitere Komponente nahtlos angelegt, jene der textilen Tiefe. In der Regel geben die einen Schnüre, Fäden oder Garne eine primäre Struktur vor, in welche die zweite, sekundäre eingeflochten wird. Die beiden Systeme sind tiefengestaffelt erkennbar und oftmals durch strukturelle oder farbliche Unterschiede im Resultat ersichtlich. Dieses einfache Prinzip hat über eine unmittelbare Konstruktionslogik hinaus Konsequenzen in der Textur und Haptik des Gewebes. Seit jeher ist der Mensch daran gewöhnt und schätzt das

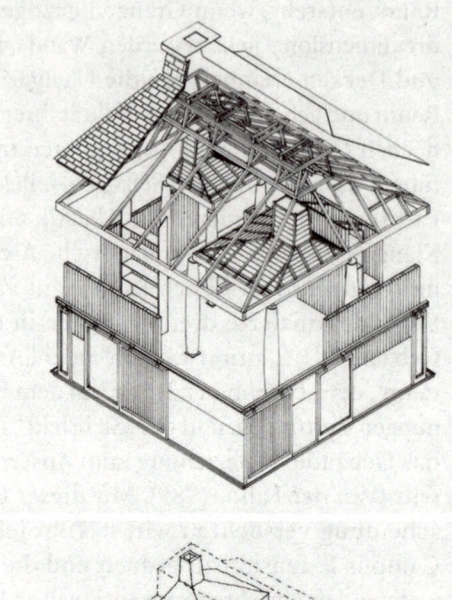

1, 2 Orinda House, Charles W. Moore, San Francisco, 1962: Interieur, Axonometrie, Konzeptskizze. Orinda House, Charles W. Moore, San Francisco, 1962: interior, axonometric drawing, conceptual sketch.

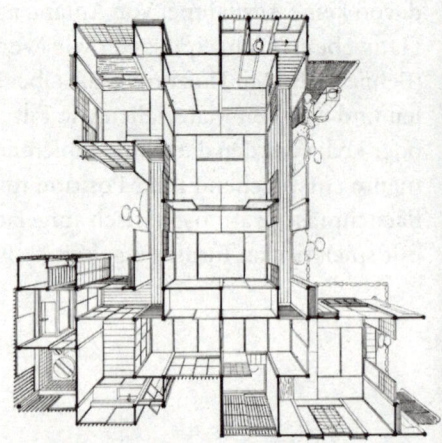

3 Teilung und Ordnung im Japanischen Wohnhaus, Tetsuro Yoshida, „Das Japanische Wohnhaus", 1954. Division and order in the Japanese house, Tetsuro Yoshida, *Das japanische Wohnhaus* (The Japanese House and Garden), [1935] 1954.

Raum im Raum

Space is created when boundaries are drawn and defined in three dimensions. Walls, floors and ceilings allow us to navigate through space while adding qualities and atmosphere through the tactility of their surfaces. They shape light and shadow, reflect colour tones and define the acoustics and sound of the rooms. The Dutch architect and Benedictine monk Dom Hans van der Laan identified three scales of space in relation to buildings: the intimate zone of the 'workspace'; the 'walking-space', in which social encounters take place; and the 'visual field', in which a building enters into a relationship with the exterior space (Van der Laan 1977). With this distinction in mind, we set out to organise the Campus Extension project and conceptually clarify its intrinsic intent. Walls, room dividers, screens, lattice frames and hanging structures would be employed as elements that structure the neutral interior spatial network.

In human culture, according to Adolf Behne, the *practical* is inextricably linked to the *play instinct*. 'Primitive man […] demonstrates his instinct for play even in his tools, which he makes smooth and beautiful beyond the demands of strict necessity, painting them or decorating them with ornaments. The tool called "house" is no exception to this. From the very beginning the house has been as much a toy as a tool' (Behne 1926, p. 1). Using wooden boards, rods and slats, as well as soft materials such as felt, fabrics and leather, the space-defining elements were atmospherically charged with surface presence according to their position and joined together using playful intuition [figs. 1, 2].

The role of the wall

Thus, walls are used to carve space into defined units, dividing it into spatial containers that communicate with each other via openings. The wall element becomes a door, a sliding wall, is opened, folded, rotated and opens or closes rooms. Building the walls in Ebaholz required a system that would enable a whole set of spatial variations. The system used made it possible to design spaces flexibly and according to the requirements of the users while allowing them to 'contract and expand' as desired, as described by Gaston Bachelard in his *Poetics of Space* (Bachelard 1958, p. 51).

At least since modern architecture proclaimed, over a hundred years ago, that the wall as a spatial boundary should be liberated from its load-bearing function, it has been freed from its static function in the building's structural frame and has been able to concentrate on its innate role of defining space. Since then, the wall has always behaved like a backdrop, something in the background, allowing the protagonists of the room—stairs, furniture and above all the people as figures in the space—to play their part in everyday dramas. However, we should not underestimate the wall in its own importance as a carrier not only of spatial information, but also as a material presence. This was completely negated in the purge of functionalism, thus turning the wall into a pale canvas, light in colour, flat and as smooth as possible.

The wall, however, has always had an entirely different depth to it, something that is already present in the word itself. The German word for wall, *Wand*, refers back to *Gewand*, meaning *garment* and thus to a light textile covering, pointing back in time to its origins as a tent. The first human dwellings, after the

Zugängliche dieser Stofflichkeit. Das Kleid des Raums ist durchaus nahe an der menschlichen Bekleidung. Deren Tiefe und Schichtung—je näher am Körper, desto feiner das Gewebe, je weiter aussen, desto robuster und grober, aber auch impermeabler—schützen das verletzliche Wesen.

Diese Tiefe, welche uns im Bereich der Kleidung vollkommen natürlich und funktional erscheint, ist der architektonischen Wand heute vollkommen abhandengekommen. Mit dem Siegeszug der Gipskartonplattensysteme wurden die Wände zu einer glatt verschliffenen Abstraktion degradiert, die im Streiflicht absolute Perfektion für den finalen Farbauftrag demonstrieren müssen. Wie weit von den stofflichen Ursprüngen hat sich das heutige Bauen damit entfernt! Die Schattenseite der abgeglätteten Leichtbauwände ist aber deren statische Natur und die Unmöglichkeit der Flexibilität und Demontierbarkeit. Eine Gipswand kann nicht versetzt werden, sie muss abgebrochen und unwiederbringlich zerstört werden. Die Metallständer wandern ins Altmetall, die Gipskartonplatten können nur noch zerkleinert und entsorgt werden. Damit wird das Leichtbauelement de facto zum unverrückbaren Bauteil.

Textile Tiefe

„Die Abspaltung der Konstruktion von der materiellen und handwerklichen Realität macht aus Architektur ein Bühnenbild für das Auge, eine blosse Szenographie, die weder Material noch Konstruktion die notwendige Authenzität verleihen. Der Sinn für die ‹Aura›, für die Macht der Anwesenheit, wie sie Walter Benjamin für jedes authentische Kunstwerk als notwendig erachtete, ist verloren gegangen" (Pallasmaa, 2013). Diesem Verlust an Tiefe versuchten wir im Projekt Ebaholz zu begegnen. Wie nimmt man die Beziehung der Teile im Raum wahr? Gibt es Gestaltungsmotive, die eine Durchgängigkeit und Lesbarkeit erlauben, oder werden Widersprüche und Kontraste erarbeitet, welche Spannungen erzeugen? Die Studierenden waren gefordert, aus der Logik von einzelnen, greifbaren Teilen eine ganze Systematik zu entwickeln, die alle Teile des Raums umfassen und eine breite Palette von Raumübergängen meistern kann. Neben dem regulären Wandmodul und einfachen Türen oder Doppeltüren sollten die grösseren Räume um die Aula flexibel definiert und in mehreren Zuständen erlebt werden können. Im täglichen Gebrauch werden sie Teil einer offenen Zirkulation, im Falle von Vorlesungen wird Konzentration und Ruhe erforderlich. Diese Räume sollten atmen und auf einfache Weise mit Mehrfachnutzen überlagert werden können [Abb. 4].

Alle Wände sollten in Elementen herstellbar und jederzeit demontierbar sein. Damit sind die Positionen für Anpassungen offen, die Räume können mühelos erweitert oder auch unterteilt werden. Die Konstruktion als Holzbauwände mit geschraubten, demontablen Verbindungen war damit naheliegend. Über diesen Grundsatz hinaus sollten weitere Aspekte in die Gestaltung der Oberflächen aufgenommen werden, allem voran Akustik, aber auch Materialität, Rhythmus und Farbigkeit. Dies nicht zuletzt, um dem Rohbau aus schalungsglattem Beton eine behagliche Komponente entgegenzusetzen.

Die Wand als Objekt verlangt nach Hülle und Struktur. Das, was gegen aussen den Ausdruck herstellt, muss in einer logischen Art und Weise aufgebaut und gehalten werden. Inneres und Äusseres bedingen sich, aber sind nicht deckungsgleich, sondern müssen sich

caves and weightiness of other earthworks, were the tents of the nomads that needed to be transportable, foldable or rollable, and above all light in weight. Primitive methods of manufacturing textiles satisfied this need well, as Gottfried Semper notes when referring to their origin in *Der Stil* (Semper 1860). Knotting and weaving techniques made it possible to produce not only carpets, but also blankets, wall hangings and even fences. In this way, enclosures could be erected as well as tents, yurts and mobile dwellings in general [fig. 3].

Dressing the space

At the same time, these light, soft, enveloping elements required a supporting structural frame, be it the scissor lattices of the yurts or light supporting skeletons made from tent poles. This was an early anticipation of the modernist call to separate the structural and space-defining functions of walls, which developed naturally within the construction logic of ephemeral building. The weaving, knotting and binding of the lightweight walls and fabric partitions seamlessly incorporate another component, that of textile depth. As a rule, one cord, thread or yarn precedes a primary structure into which the second, supplemental structure is woven. The two systems are recognisable in terms of depth and are often visible through structural or colour differences in the finished element. This simple principle has consequences for the texture and feel of the fabric that go beyond the immediate logic of construction. Humans have always been accustomed to and appreciated the accessibility of this materiality. The 'dressing' of the space is thus very closely aligned with human clothing. Its depth and layering — the closer to the body, the finer the fabric; the further out, the more robust and coarser, but also more impermeable — protect the vulnerable being within.

This depth, which seems completely natural and functional in the realm of clothing, has been completely lost in today's architectural walls. With the triumphant advance of plasterboard systems, walls have been degraded to smoothly sanded abstractions that, in the raking light, must demonstrate absolute perfection for the final application of paint. How far modern building has strayed from its material origins! However, the downside of smoothed, lightweight walls is their static nature and the impossibility of flexibility and dismantling. A plaster wall cannot be moved — it has to be demolished and irretrievably destroyed. The metal studs end up as scrap metal, the plasterboard panels can only be shredded and disposed of. This makes the lightweight construction element de facto an immovable component.

Textile depth

'The detachment of construction from the realities of matter and craft further turns architecture into stage sets for the eye, into a scenography devoid of the authenticity of matter and construction. The sense of "aura", the authority of presence, that Walter Benjamin regards as a necessary quality for an authentic piece of art, has been lost' (Pallasmaa 1996, p. 25). In the Ebaholz project, we set out to counter this loss of depth. How do you perceive the relationship of the elements in space? Are there design motifs that allow for continuity and legibility, or are contradictions and contrasts created that generate tension? The students were challenged to develop an entire system from the logic of individual, tangible pieces that encompasses

gegenseitig stärken. Die Konstruktion der Objekte verlangte nach einer intensiven Arbeit mit dem Material. Bretter, Latten und Platten zeigen sich in ihren Eigenheiten, mit ihren Kanten und Ecken, und sollten auf inspirierende Weise zueinanderkommen. Materialprototypen zeigten Übergänge, Stufen, Absätze und Ecksituationen auf und wurden parallel zeichnerisch mit Axonometrien und präzisen Schnittzeichnungen ergänzt [Abb. 5].

Das schliesslich vom Studio erarbeitete Wandsystem bietet eine vielfältige Lösung an. Ein Kern aus Holzwerkstoffplatten, welcher Stabilität und Dichtigkeit garantiert, wurde beidseitig mit Tafeln aus massiver Weisstanne in einem geometrisch frei rhythmisierten Muster belegt. Dazwischen sind mit Schafwolle hinterlegte und über Rahmen gespannte Filzflächen als Akustikabsorber angebracht. Vier unterschiedliche Filzfarben geben über die warme Farbigkeit hinaus eine Orientierung im Gebäude mit den je Geschoss unterschiedlich verlaufenden roten Feldern, eine Referenz an das Rot, das im Campusgebäude in der Fensterfarbe wie auch im Uni-Logo präsent ist. Damit ist der Innenausbau klar als von der Hülle und dem Rohbau unabhängiger Eingriff erkennbar und von vielschichtigem, textilem Charakter. Die Wände sind adaptibel, jederzeit für Anpassungen verschiebbar und lassen, im Speziellen im Aulabereich durch den Einsatz von Schiebewandelementen, flexible Raumfiguren zu.

Die Maschinerie des Raums

Treppen bringen den Raum in Gang, verbinden und geben Anlass, sich im Gehen zu orientieren, innezuhalten und zurückzublicken. Wie Josef Frank in seinem berückenden Vergleich von Bau und Stadt festhielt, wird „das Haus als

4   Textil formulierte Raumhülle: Gregory Farmhouse, William Wurster, Santa Cruz, California, 1929. Textile-formulated spatial envelope: Gregory Farmhouse, William Wurster, Santa Cruz, California, 1929.

5   Zusammenarbeit in der Zimmermannsarbeit, in: „Encyclopédie ou dictionnaire raisonné des sciences, des arts et des métiers", 1751–1765. Carpenters working in collaboration, from: *Encyclopédie ou dictionnaire raisonné des sciences, des arts et des métiers*, 1751–1765.

all parts of the space and can master a wide range of spatial transitions. In addition to the regular wall module and single or double doors, the larger rooms around the auditorium were to be flexibly defined and experienced in several different states. In daily use, they become part of an open circulation; in the case of lectures, concentration and quiet are required. These spaces should breathe and be easily overlaid with multiple uses [fig. 4].

All walls should be constructed in modules that could be dismantled at any time. This allowed for spaces that were open to adjustments and rooms that could be easily expanded or subdivided. Building with timber walls using bolted, demountable connections was therefore an obvious choice. In addition to this principle, further aspects were to be incorporated into the design of the surfaces, primarily acoustics, but also materiality, rhythm and colour. This was not least to create an element of cosiness to contrast the smooth concrete shell.

To function as an object, a wall requires a covering and structure. That which creates the outward expression must be built and maintained in a logical manner. The interior and exterior are interdependent, but are not identical; rather, they must reinforce each other. The construction of the wall elements required intensive work with the materials. Wooden boards, slats and panels each exhibit their own characteristics, such as their edges and corners, and should join together in an inspiring way. Material prototypes demonstrated transitions, stairs, landings and corner situations, and were complemented by axonometric drawings and precise cross-sectional drawings [fig. 5].

The wall system that was ultimately developed by the studio provides a versatile solution. The core of engineered-wood panels, which guaranteed stability and impermeability, was covered on both sides with panels of solid silver fir in a geometric free-form pattern. In between, felt surfaces backed with sheep's wool and stretched over frames were employed as acoustic absorbers. In addition to the warm colour scheme, four different felt colours provide orientation within the building by means of varying red fields on each floor, a reference to the red found in the windows of the campus buildings as well as the university logo. The interior fit-out with its multilayered, textile character is thus clearly recognisable as an intervention that is independent of the exterior shell. The walls are adaptable, can be moved at any time for adjustments and allow for flexible room configurations, especially in the auditorium area through the use of sliding wall elements.

The machinery of space

Staircases set space in motion, connect it and provide an opportunity to orientate oneself, to pause and look back while walking. As Josef Frank noted in his enchanting comparison of building and city, 'The House as Path and Place', a is only brought to life by people in motion. 'A well-ordered house should be laid out like a city, with streets and alleys that lead inevitably to places that are cut off from traffic, so that one can rest there. [...] A well-laid-out house is comparable to one of those beautiful old cities, in which even a stranger immediately knows his way around and can find the city hall and the market square without having to ask' (Frank 1931, p. 146). As a central element of movement, the staircase serves, for both resident and visitor, as a spine, orchestrating the spaces around it while weaving their interplay into an inner cosmos. The path from the street via the

Weg und Platz" vom Menschen in Bewegung erst belebt. „Ein gut organisiertes Haus ist wie eine Stadt anzulegen mit Strassen und Wegen, die zwangsläufig zu Plätzen führen, welche vom Verkehr ausgeschaltet sind, so dass man auf ihnen ausruhen kann. (...) Ein gut angelegtes Haus gleicht jenen schönen alten Städten, in denen sich selbst der Fremde sofort auskennt und, ohne danach zu fragen, Rathaus und Marktplatz findet." (Frank, 1931) Als zentrales Element der Bewegung dient die Treppe den Bewohnernden oder Besuchenden als Rückgrat, das die räumlichen Organe um sich herum orchestriert und ihr Zusammenspiel zu einem inneren Kosmos verwebt. Der Weg von der Strasse über den Eingang in die oberen Etagen und hinauf zum Dach muss als roter Faden durch den Raum geführt und zelebriert werden. Treppen, Galerien und Durchgänge spielen dabei eine entscheidende Rolle. Man bewegt sich auf ihnen, ohne den Bewegungsfluss zu verlieren, und erkundet den Raum schlendernd, oder aber in Eile, auf dem Weg zu einem Ziel. Mit einer Abfolge von Bildern wie Filmstills oder Screenshots versuchten wir, die Bewegung einer Besucherin/eines Besuchers in das Gebäude und in seine Räume bis hin zum Blick zurück in die Landschaft zu einer kohärenten Abfolge von räumlichen Ereignissen zu strukturieren.

Bevor der Innenausbau beginnen konnte, musste als allererste Massnahme ein Deckendurchbruch aus dem bereits fertiggestellten Rohbau geschnitten werden. Dieser vertikale Ausbruch war entscheidend, um die übereinandergelegten Geschosse zu einer Einheit zusammenzufügen und die gewünschte Kommunikation zwischen den Geschossen zu etablieren. Darin sollte eine Treppe angeordnet werden, die über die blosse Verbindung zwischen den Etagen hinaus einen Ort definiert, zum Sitzen und Zuhören einlädt und als eigentliche Bühne des Alltags funktioniert. Die Treppe wurde im Laufe des Projekts zum skulpturalen Herzstück der Campus-Erweiterung, ein Ankunftsort und Magnet für den täglichen Gebrauch, um den sich im Tagesverlauf die unterschiedlichsten Bewegungen und die vielfältigsten Begegnungen ergeben können. In ihrer handwerklichen Herstellungsweise erzeugt sie zusammen mit den Wänden einen atmosphärisch starken Gegenpol zur neutralen Hülle des als Bürogebäude erstellten Zweckbaus und einen attraktiven Hintergrund für die tägliche Arbeit im Räderwerk der Universität.

Lehren und lernen

Im Rahmen des innovativen und praxisorientierten Entwurfsstudios Campus Extension wurde der Innenausbau in der Campus-Erweiterung Ebaholz in einem rollenden Prozess gemeinsam mit Studierenden und Spezialisten entwickelt und realisiert. Charakteristisch für diesen Ansatz ist, dass das Endergebnis nicht von Beginn an feststeht, sondern sich sukzessive im Verlauf des gestalterischen und konstruktiven Prozesses entfaltet und somit alle Akteure vom Anfang bis zum Ende miteinbezieht. Durch diesen dynamischen Entwurfs- und Bauprozess werden die Studierenden aktiv in die Planung und Umsetzung eingebunden, wodurch ein partizipativer Lern- und Erfahrungsraum entsteht. Ein essenzieller Bestandteil dieses Konzepts ist die enge Kooperation mit regionalen Handwerksbetrieben. Diese Zusammenarbeit stellt nicht nur eine Bereicherung des Projekts dar, sondern ermöglicht auch die direkte Weitergabe aktuellen handwerklichen Wissens an die Studierenden.

entrance to the upper floors then up to the roof must be guided and celebrated as a common thread running through the space. For this, stairs, galleries and passageways play a decisive role. One moves along them without losing the flow of movement, exploring the space either in a leisurely stroll or in a hurry, en route to one's destination. Using a sequence of images akin to film stills or screenshots, we attempted to structure the visitors' movement into the building and through its spaces, right up to the view looking back into the landscape, into a coherent sequence of spatial events.

Before the interior work could begin, the very first step was to cut an opening in the floor of the already-completed shell. This vertical cut-out was crucial for merging the stacked floors into a single unit and establishing the desired communication between the storeys. The staircase installed in this space was meant to do more than merely connect the floors, but rather to invite people to sit and listen, thus functioning like a literal stage for everyday life. Over the course of the project, the staircase became the sculptural centrepiece of the campus extension, a place of arrival and a magnet for daily use, around which a wide variety of movement and encounters can take place throughout the day. Together with the walls, the handcrafted design of the staircase creates a strong atmospheric counterpoint to the neutral shell of the functional office building and an attractive backdrop for the daily work of the university's operations.

Teaching and learning

As part of the innovative and practice-oriented Campus Extension design studio, the interior fit-out of the Ebaholz campus extension was developed and realised in a rolling process together with students and outside specialists. One hallmark of this approach is that the end result is not predetermined at the outset but evolves gradually over the course of the design and construction process, involving all stakeholders from start to finish. Through this dynamic design and construction process, students are actively involved in the planning and realisation, creating a participatory space for learning and experience. An essential component of this concept is the close cooperation with regional skilled-trade contractors. This collaboration not only enriches the project but also enables the direct transfer of up-to-date artisanal knowledge and skills to the students.

This direct connection between theory and practice reflects an understanding of education based on independent learning through direct experience—a principle already emphasised by Josef Albers at the Bauhaus: 'Learning is better than teaching because it is *more intensive*: the more we teach, the less students can learn' (Albers 1928). By engaging in both design and craft, students gain not only technical knowledge, but also a deeper understanding of materials, construction and the many processes involved in building.

The rolling process as a method

For over 20 years, the rolling process has shaped the methodical approach to the development and implementation of full-scale (1:1) activities with students at the Craft & Structure unit at the School of Architecture at the University of Liechtenstein. This method began with small, ephemeral material experiments during summer workshops, developed into the first permanent construction projects such as the

In dieser direkten Verknüpfung von Theorie und Praxis spiegelt sich ein Bildungsverständnis wider, das auf eigenständigem Lernen durch unmittelbare Erfahrung basiert — ein Prinzip, das bereits Josef Albers am Bauhaus betonte: „Lernen ist besser, weil intensiver als lehren: je mehr gelehrt wird, desto weniger kann gelernt werden." (Albers, 1928) Indem Studierende sowohl gestalterisch als auch handwerklich tätig werden, erlangen sie nicht nur technisches Wissen, sondern auch ein tieferes Verständnis für Materialität, Konstruktion und die Prozesse des Bauens.

Der rollende Prozess als Methode

Der rollende Prozess prägt seit über zwanzig Jahren die methodische Herangehensweise bei der Entwicklung und Umsetzung von 1:1-Aktivitäten mit Studierenden am Craft & Structure Unit an der School of Architecture der Universität Liechtenstein. Diese Methode begann mit kleinen, ephemeren Materialexperimenten während Sommer-Workshops, entwickelte sich weiter zu ersten permanenten Bauprojekten wie der *Loipahütte* und führte schliesslich zu grösseren Bauaufgaben, darunter die *Modellwerkstatt* und aktuell die Campus-Erweiterung Ebaholz. Derzeit wird mit Studierenden der *Red Cube*, ein Kiosk für die Universität, entworfen, entwickelt und gebaut.

Ein zentrales Element dieses Prozesses sind wöchentliche Besprechungen zwischen Studierenden und Lehrenden, in denen Konzepte und Entwürfe kontinuierlich diskutiert und weiterentwickelt werden. Die Studierenden arbeiten in kleinen Teams, analog zur Zusammenarbeit in der späteren architektonischen Praxis, und übernehmen spezifische Aufgabenbereiche. Diese interaktive Arbeitsweise gleicht einem „Pingpongspiel", das sich bis zum Abschluss des Projekts fortsetzt.

Ein wesentlicher Bestandteil des rollenden Prozesses als Methode des Bauens im Massstab 1:1 mit Studierenden ist die enge Kooperation mit regionalen Handwerksbetrieben. Diese Zusammenarbeit ermöglicht es den Studierenden, unmittelbar von handwerklichem Wissen zu profitieren und traditionelle sowie zeitgenössische Techniken praxisnah zu erlernen. Darüber hinaus fördert dieser Austausch eine gemeinsame Entwicklungskultur innerhalb der jeweiligen Bauaufgabe. In Anlehnung an historische Bauprozesse, in denen Wissen nicht streng in separate Disziplinen unterteilt war, sondern ein integratives Verständnis von Entwurf und Ausführung bestand, reduziert diese Methode Schnittstellenprobleme und schafft eine ganzheitliche Herangehensweise an den Bauprozess. Die Verbindung von akademischer Lehre und handwerklicher Praxis trägt somit nicht nur zur fachlichen Ausbildung der Studierenden bei, sondern stärkt auch interdisziplinäre Kompetenzen und ein vertieftes Verständnis für den Bau als kollaborativen Prozess.

In diesem Sinne sind Entwerfen und Bauen als gleichwertige Prozesse zu verstehen — ähnlich der mittelalterlichen Bauhütte, in der Planung und Umsetzung untrennbar miteinander verbunden waren. Anstatt einer starren Trennung zwischen Entwurf und Realisierung folgt der Prozess einer lebendigen, adaptiven und forschenden Entwicklung. Diese Methode erfordert ein hohes Mass an Flexibilität und Vertrauen zwischen Studierenden und Lehrenden, hat sich jedoch über die Jahre als nachhaltiges und bewährtes Konzept etabliert.

Loipahütte, a cross-country ski hut, then ultimately led to larger construction projects, including the school's own model workshop and, currently, the Ebaholz campus extension. The Red Cube, a kiosk for the university, is currently being designed, developed and built with students.

A central element of this process is weekly meetings between students and teachers at which concepts and designs are continuously discussed and developed. The students work in small teams, similar to the collaboration they might later find at an architectural practice, and take on specific areas of responsibility. This interactive method of working resembles a ping pong game that continues until the project's completion.

A key component of the rolling process as a method of building at 1:1 scale with students is close collaboration with regional skilled-trade contractors. This collaboration enables students to benefit directly from craft expertise and to learn both traditional and current techniques in a practical way. In addition, this exchange promotes a shared development culture within the respective construction task. Inspired by historical processes of building, in which knowledge was not strictly divided into separate disciplines but rather existed as an integrative understanding of design and execution, this method reduces interface problems and creates a holistic approach to the construction process. The combination of academic teaching and practical hands-on work not only contributes to the students' specialist training but also strengthens interdisciplinary skills and a deeper understanding of construction as a collaborative process.

In this sense, design and construction should be seen as equal processes—similar to the medieval masons' lodge, where design and construction were inextricably linked. Instead of a rigid separation between design and realisation, the process follows a lively, adaptive and exploratory development. This method requires a great deal of flexibility and trust between students and teachers but has established itself over the years as a sustainable and proven approach.

Montageprozess Assembly process

Erfahrungen als Bauherrenvertreter beim Ebaholz-Projekt der Universität Liechtenstein

Experiences as Client Representative for the University of Liechtenstein's Ebaholz' Project

Michael Heinzle

Die Realisierung des neuen Aussenstandorts Ebaholz als Ergänzung zum Campus der Universität Liechtenstein auf dem Spoerry-Areal stellte eine komplexe und anspruchsvolle Aufgabe dar, die eine präzise Planung und Koordination erforderte. Als Bauherrenvertreter war es meine Aufgabe, die Interessen der Universität zu wahren und sicherzustellen, dass das Projekt im Einklang mit den festgelegten Zielen und Vorgaben umgesetzt wurde. Dazu gehörte eine enge Zusammenarbeit mit Architektinnen und Architekten, Architekturstudierenden, verschiedenen Gewerken und internen Stakeholdern, um eine reibungslose Umsetzung aller Planungs- und Bauphasen zu gewährleisten. Die Koordination und die Kommunikation zwischen den verschiedenen Beteiligten waren entscheidend, um Missverständnisse und Verzögerungen zu vermeiden.

Ein besonderer Aspekt des Projekts war die enge Zusammenarbeit mit Studierenden der Liechtenstein School of Architecture, die nicht nur innovative Vorschläge für den Innenausbau einbrachten, sondern aktiv an der Entwicklung und Gestaltung der Räume beteiligt waren. Gemeinsam im Studio Meister Rist konnten wir für die Universität neue Ansätze entwickeln und direkt umsetzen. Hierfür wurden von den Studierenden zahlreiche Wandmodelle gebaut und zur Diskussion gestellt. Diese praxisnahe Kooperation ermöglichte es, die Räume bis zu einem gewissen Grad selbst zu entwickeln und gleichzeitig kreative wie nachhaltige Lösungen zu finden.

Besonders hervorzuheben ist, dass alternative Bauweisen zum herkömmlichen Trockenbau erprobt wurden, um auf den Einsatz von Gipskarton zu verzichten. Im Austausch mit den Studierenden und durch regelmässiges Feedback entstanden so nachhaltige Holzwände, die mit walisischer Schafwolle gedämmt wurden. Auch die durchdachte Farb- und Formgebung wurde gemeinsam gestaltet und findet bei den Mitarbeitenden sowie den Besuchenden der Universität grossen Anklang. Diese Zusammenarbeit zwischen Architekturstudio und Bauherrenvertretung verleiht den Räumen nicht nur einen einzigartigen Charakter, sondern macht sie zu einem Beispiel dafür, wie kreative Bildungsarbeit in der Praxis zu aussergewöhnlichen Ergebnissen führen kann.

Ein zentrales Thema des Projekts war die Balance zwischen architektonischer Ästhetik und den funktionalen Anforderungen der Nutzenden. Beispielsweise spielten Raumakustik und Flexibilität eine grosse Rolle. Die Entscheidung über die Raumaufteilung erforderte eine sorgfältige Abwägung: Ob offene Bürolandschaften oder kleinere Büroeinheiten besser geeignet wären, wurde unter Einbindung der Mitarbeitenden diskutiert. Letztlich wurde eine Mischform gewählt, die den verschiedenen Arbeitsanforderungen gerecht wird. Die beiden Seminarräume wurden so gestaltet, dass sie bei Bedarf flexibel geöffnet und zu einer grossen Fläche — einer Aula — verbunden werden können, wobei eine repräsentative Holztreppe als verbindendes Element zwischen den Stockwerken dient. Um den Anforderungen der modernen Lehre gerecht zu werden, sind die Seminarräume zudem für hybride Lernformate ausgestattet.

Die Integration der verschiedenen Gewerke stellte ebenfalls eine signifikante Herausforderung dar. Die Koordination von Rohbau, Elektroinstallation und Innenausstattung erforderte eine präzise Abstimmung, um Verzögerungen und Kostenüberschreitungen zu vermeiden. Besonders anspruchsvoll war die Implementierung moderner Gebäudetechnik.

Erfahrungen als Bauherrenvertreter

As an extension to the University of Liechtenstein campus, the construction of the new Ebaholz satellite facility on the Spoerry site was a complex and challenging task that required precise planning and coordination. As the client's representative, my role was to protect the University's interests while ensuring that the project was implemented in accordance with the defined objectives and specifications. This involved close collaboration with the architects, architecture students, various trades and internal stakeholders to ensure the smooth execution and completion of all planning and construction phases. Coordination and communication between the diverse parties involved was key to avoiding misunderstandings and delays.

One special aspect of the project was the close collaboration with students from the Liechtenstein School of Architecture, who not only provided innovative proposals for the interior work but also took an active role in the development and design of the spaces. Working together in the Meister Rist studio, we were able to develop and directly implement new approaches for the University. To this end, the students built numerous wall models and presented them for discussion. This practical, hands-on collaboration allowed us to develop the spaces to a certain extent, while seeking and finding creative and sustainable solutions.

It is particularly worth noting that we explored alternative construction methods to conventional drywall construction in order to avoid the use of plasterboard. Through dialogue and regular feedback with the students, we developed a sustainable wooden wall system insulated with Valais sheep wool. The carefully considered colour scheme and formal design were also a collaborative effort and have proved popular with staff and visitors to the University. This collaboration between the architecture studio and the client's representative not only gives the spaces a unique character but also makes them an example of how creative educational work can lead to exceptional results in the real world.

A central theme of the project was the balance between architectural aesthetics and the functional needs of the users. For example, the acoustic qualities and flexible use of the spaces played a major role. Deciding on the spatial organisation required careful consideration: With the involvement of the building's staff, we discussed whether open-plan office landscapes or smaller office units would be more appropriate. Ultimately, a hybrid form was chosen that fulfils the various work requirements. The two seminar rooms have been designed to be flexible, allowing them to be opened up and combined into one large room — an auditorium — when required, with an impressive wooden staircase serving as the connecting element between the floors. To meet the demands of modern teaching, the seminar rooms are also equipped for hybrid learning formats.

Integrating the various building trades also posed a significant challenge. The coordination of the core and shell, electrical and interior fit-out work required precise coordination to avoid delays and cost overruns. The implementation of modern building services was particularly demanding. Collaboration with skilled specialists and regular progress reviews were essential.

Time management was critical to the success of the project. The vacating of existing premises and the temporary relocation of staff, both on campus and at home, required careful

Die Zusammenarbeit mit spezialisierten Fachkräften und die regelmässige Überprüfung der Fortschritte waren hierbei unerlässlich.

Das Zeitmanagement war ein kritischer Faktor für den Projekterfolg. Die Auflösung bestehender Liegenschaften und die temporäre Unterbringung der Mitarbeitenden am Campus und im Homeoffice erforderten eine sorgfältige Planung und Koordination, um den Übergang reibungslos zu gestalten und den laufenden Betrieb der Universität nicht zu beeinträchtigen. Hierzu war eine enge Abstimmung mit den betroffenen Abteilungen und eine flexible Anpassung an unvorhergesehene Ereignisse notwendig.

Auch die Einhaltung des vorgegebenen Budgets war von zentraler Bedeutung. Durch eine detaillierte Planung und kontinuierliche Kostenüberwachung konnte sichergestellt werden, dass das Projekt innerhalb der finanziellen Vorgaben blieb. Regelmässige Abstimmungen mit den Finanzverantwortlichen und eine strikte Kontrolle aller Ausgaben waren essenziell. Die Identifizierung von Einsparpotenzialen sowie Verhandlungen mit Zuliefernden sowie Dienstleistenden trugen ebenfalls zur erfolgreichen Budgeteinhaltung bei.

Ein weiterer wichtiger Aspekt des Projekts war die Integration von Nachhaltigkeits- und Innovationsaspekten. Die Planung und Umsetzung energieeffizienter Lösungen und der Einsatz erneuerbarer Energien standen im Fokus. Dies umfasste die Installation einer Photovoltaikanlage durch die Gebäudeeigentümer, die Implementierung intelligenter Gebäudemanagementsysteme sowie den Einbau energieeffizienter Beleuchtungskörper.

Insgesamt stellte das Ebaholz-Projekt eine wertvolle Erfahrung dar, die es ermöglichte, einen bedeutenden Beitrag zur Weiterentwicklung der Universität Liechtenstein zu leisten. Die erfolgreiche Umsetzung des Projekts zeigt, dass durch sorgfältige Planung, enge Zusammenarbeit und eine kontinuierliche Überwachung der Fortschritte auch komplexe Bauvorhaben erfolgreich realisiert werden können. Der neue Standort Ebaholz bietet nun moderne und nachhaltige Räumlichkeiten, die den Anforderungen der Universität und ihrer Nutzenden gerecht werden und eine optimale Umgebung für Lehre, Forschung und Administration schaffen.

planning and coordination to ensure a smooth transition with no disruption to the University's ongoing operations. This required close liaison with the affected departments and flexible adaption to unforeseen events.

Adherence to the established budget was also key. Detailed planning and continuous cost monitoring ensured that the project remained within the financial constraints. Regular coordination with financial managers and strict monitoring of expenditures were essential. Identifying potential savings and negotiating with suppliers and service providers also contributed to successful budget compliance.

Another important aspect of the project was the integration of sustainability and innovation considerations. The focus was on planning and implementing energy-efficient solutions and using renewable energy. This included the installation of a photovoltaic system by the building owners, the implementation of intelligent building management systems and the provision of energy-efficient lighting fixtures.

All in all, the Ebaholz project has been a valuable experience that has contributed significantly to the further development of the University of Liechtenstein. The successful completion of the project demonstrates that even complex construction projects can be fully and effectively executed through diligent planning, close collaboration and continuous progress monitoring. The new 'Ebaholz' site now offers modern and sustainable facilities that meet the needs of the University and its users and creates an optimal environment for teaching, research and administration.

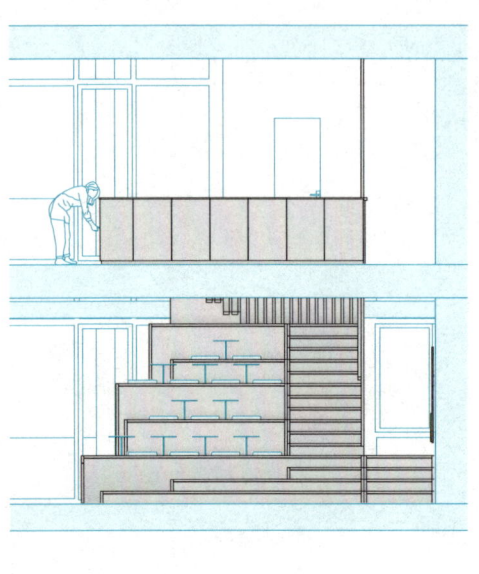
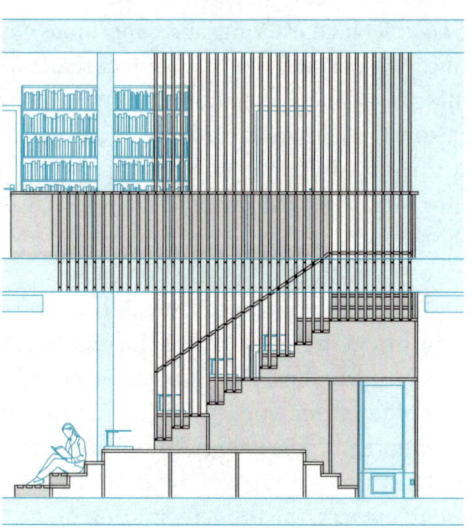
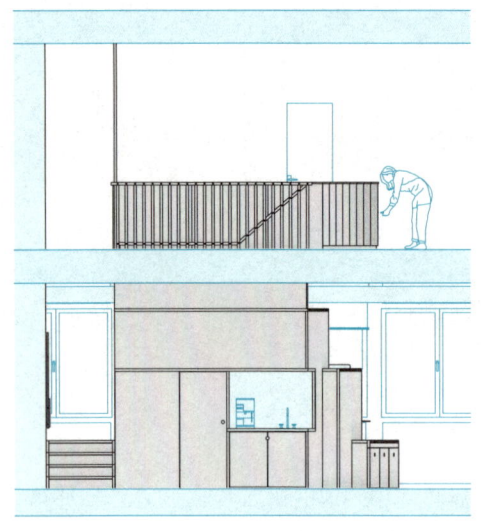
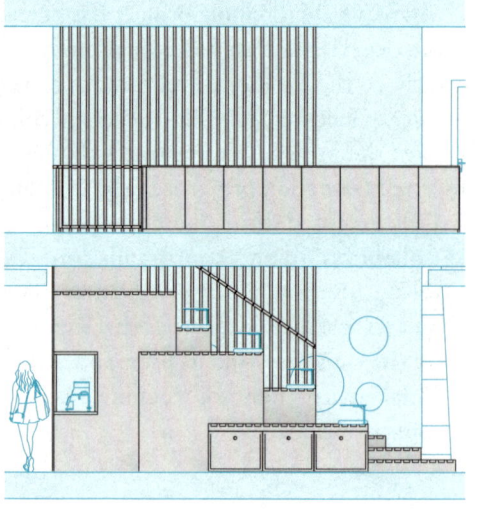

Ausführungspläne Construction drawings

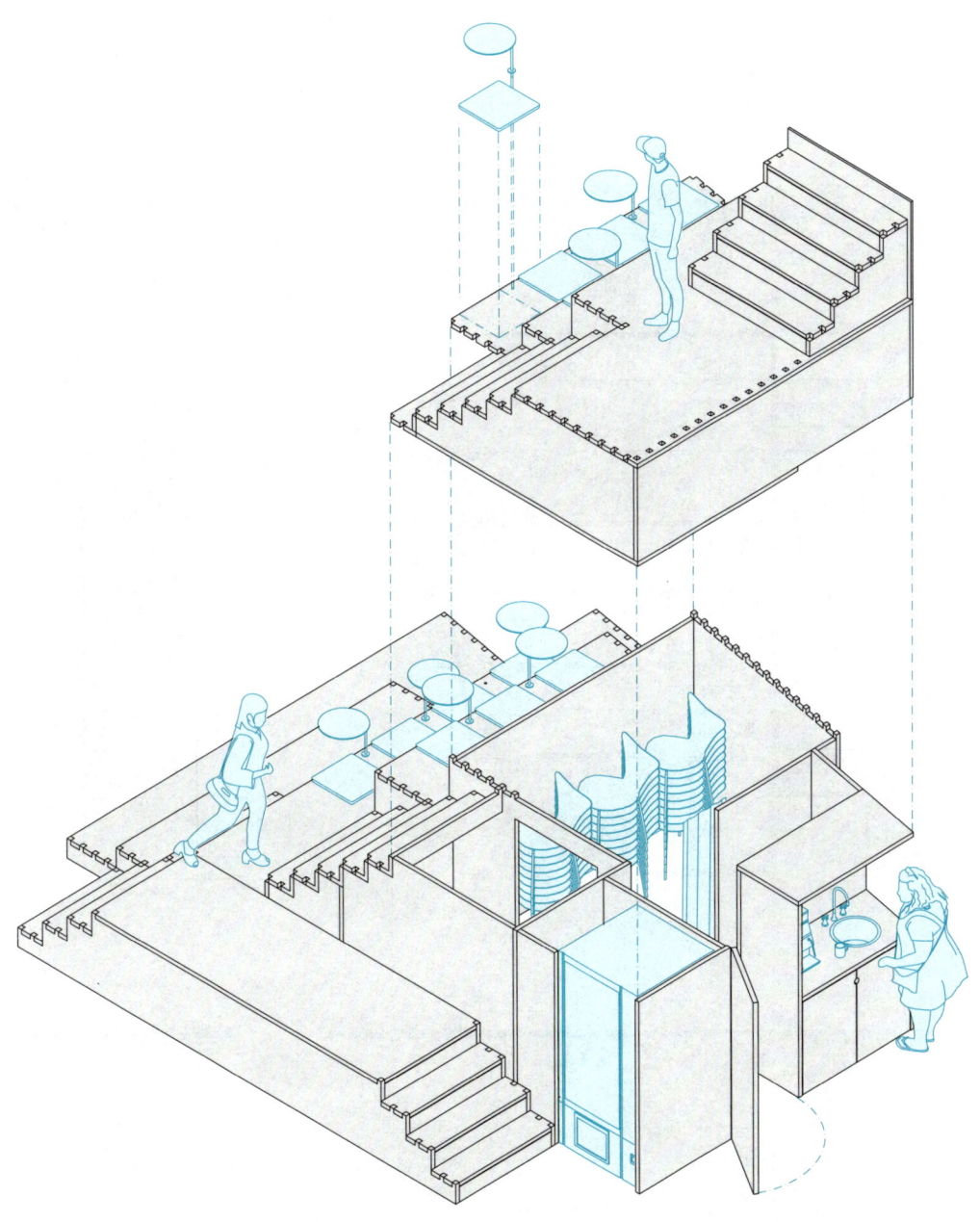

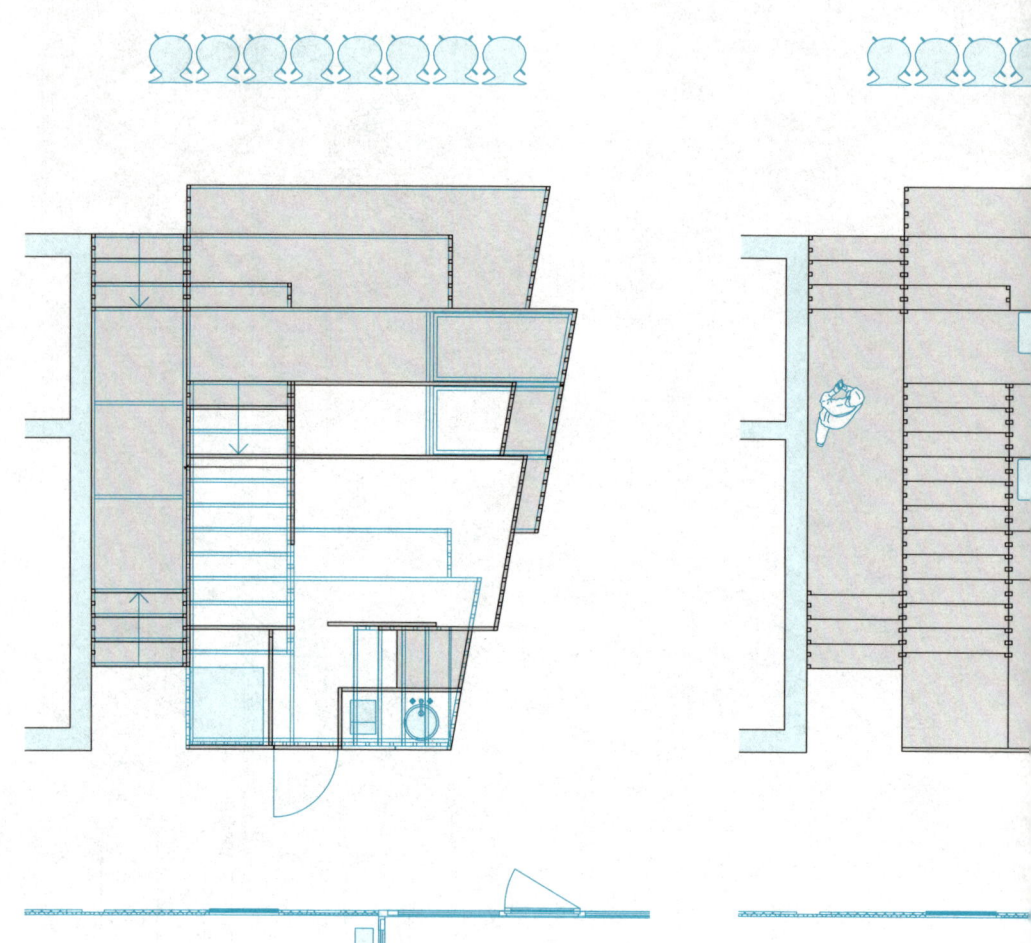

Ausführungspläne Construction drawings

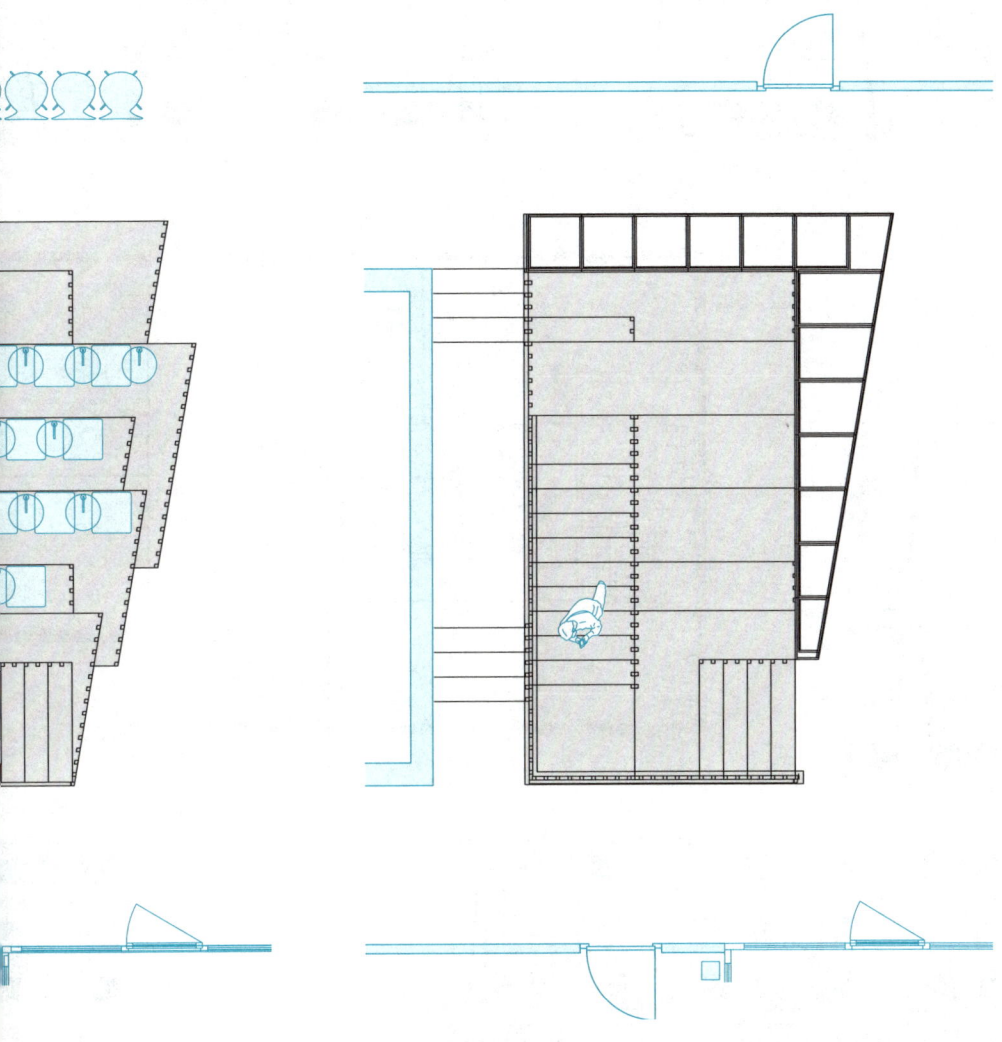

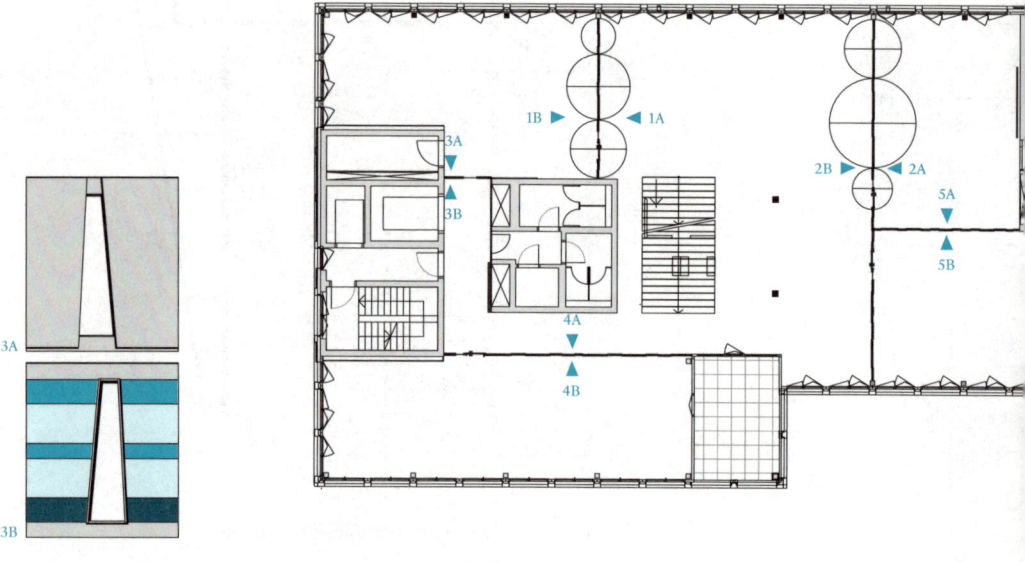

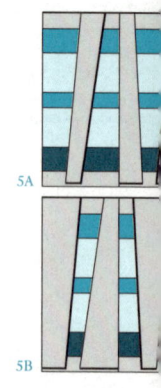

Ausführungspläne Construction drawings

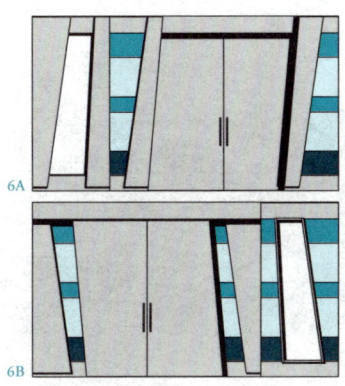
6A

6B

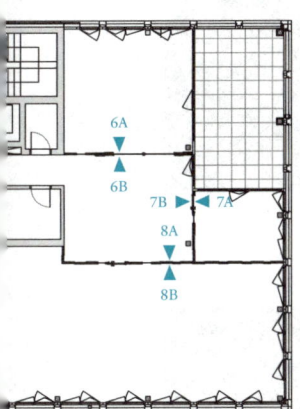

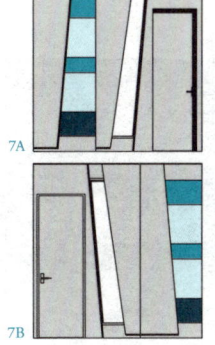
7A

7B

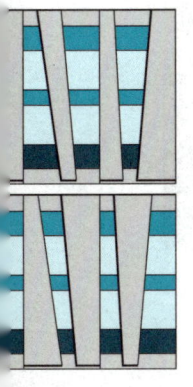

8A

8B

Ort der Begegnung Space for exchange

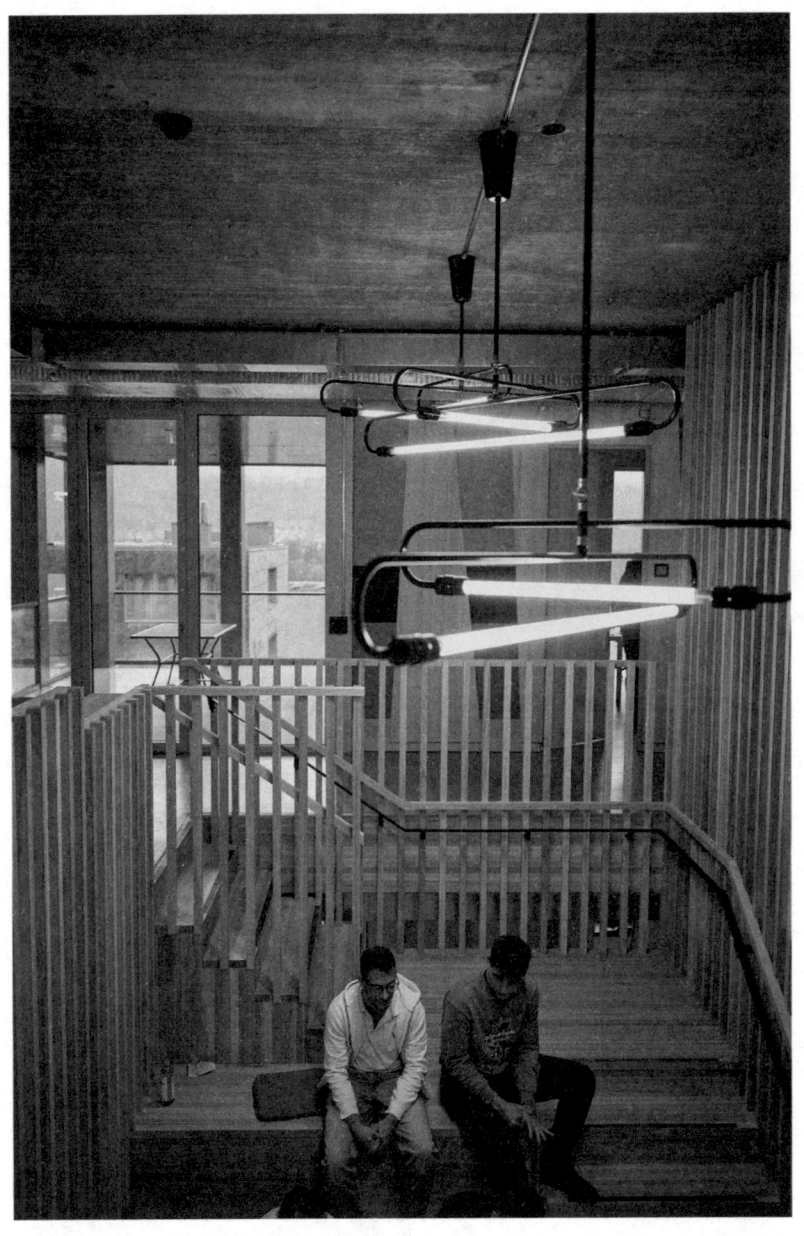

Factbox
Fact Box

Ebaholz Campus-Erweiterung

Zeitraum	Oktober 2022 bis Juni 2023
Ort	Vaduz, Liechtenstein
Bauherrschaft	Universität Liechtenstein, School of Architecture
Partner	Frommelt Zimmerei und Ing. Holzbau AG, Schaan, Liechtenstein

Realisierung durch Studierende des Advanced Studios Craft & Structure in Kooperation mit der Frommelt Zimmerei und Ing. Holzbau AG, Schaan, Liechtenstein.

Nachhaltigkeitskette, Entwurfsarbeit und Ausführung mit Studierenden sowie lokalen Zimmerleuten und weiteren Handwerkern.

Technische Beschreibung

Ausführung des Innenausbaus in Leichtbauweise
- Böden in Anhydrit und Hartbeton (Duschen) geschliffen und versiegelt
- Erschliessung Elektro und Netzwerk mit Bodendosen, Leitungsführung in Dämmebene
- Innenwände: Sichtseiten in Weisstanne, massiv, Filzlagen auf Rahmen gespannt und mit Schafwolle hinterfüllt, Mittellagen in MDF, Bürotüren und Dreh-Schiebetüren mit Verkleidung in Weisstanne, massiv
- Treppenmöbel: Stufen, Sitzflächen und Lamellengitter in Esche, massiv, Handlauf in Stahl, lackiert
- Küchenmöbel: Sichtfronten in Eschenfurnier auf MDF, Innenverkleidungen in Kunstharz

Entwurf und Realisierung

Universität Liechtenstein, Vaduz, School of Architecture

Dozierende
Carmen Rist-Stadelmann, Urs Meister

Studierende Advanced Studio Craft & Structure
Meister – Rist-Stadelmann WS 2022–2023
Ada Selinay, Arroyave Laura, Bertoni Rafaela, Dablander Pia Luisa, Dietz Francis, Flick Leonard-Vinzenz, Hagen Magdalena, Juen Franz-Felix, Kosec Kim, Lindner Sara, Mack Luis Frank, Reinprecht Leon, Stoll Sara, Strimmer Luca, Yavuz Asli

Studierende Advanced Studio Craft & Structure
Meister – Rist-Stadelmann SS 2023
Ada Selinay, Akman Ebru, Bacinski Aleksandar, Beck Cosima, Bösch Michelle, Breitruck Sophie Marie Luise, Defranceschi Patricia Clara, Derdelen Derin, Dünser Stefanie, Glushko Alexander, Maksic Stefania, Nachbaur Magdalena, Neurauter Leah, Tan Tugba, Ünsal Kader, Winkelmann Valérie, Yavuz Asli

Ebaholz Campus Extension

Time period	October 2022 – June 2023
Place	Vaduz, Liechtenstein
Client	University of Liechtenstein, School of Architecture
Partner	Frommelt Zimmerei und Ing. Holzbau AG, Schaan, Liechtenstein

Realisation with students of the Advanced Studio Craft & Structure in cooperation with Frommelt Zimmerei und Ing. Holzbau AG, Schaan, Liechtenstein.

Sustainability chain from design to execution, with students doing the work with the help of local carpenters and craftspeople.

Technical description

Execution of the interior fit-out in lightweight construction
- Floors of anhydrite and granolithic cement (showers) screed, ground and sealed
- Electrical and network connections with floor boxes, cable routing in the insulation layer
- Interior partitions: exposed surfaces of solid silver fir, felt layers mounted on frames and padded with sheep's wool, middle layers of MDF, office doors and swinging/sliding doors with panelling of solid fir
- Staircase element: solid ash steps, seats and louvre grilles, lacquered steel handrail
- Kitchen furniture: visible fronts of ash veneer on MDF, interior laminate of synthetic resin

Design and realisation

University of Liechtenstein, Vaduz, School of Architecture

Lecturers
Carmen Rist-Stadelmann, Urs Meister

Students Advanced Studio Craft & Structure
Meister – Rist-Stadelmann WS 2022–2023
Ada Selinay, Arroyave Laura, Bertoni Rafaela, Dablander Pia Luisa, Dietz Francis, Flick Leonard-Vinzenz, Hagen Magdalena, Juen Franz-Felix, Kosec Kim, Lindner Sara, Mack Luis Frank, Reinprecht Leon, Stoll Sara, Strimmer Luca, Yavuz Asli

Students Advanced Studio Craft & Structure
Meister – Rist-Stadelmann SS 2023
Ada Selinay, Akman Ebru, Bacinski Aleksandar, Beck Cosima, Bösch Michelle, Breitruck Sophie Marie Luise, Defranceschi Patricia Clara, Derdelen Derin, Dünser Stefanie, Glushko Alexander, Maksic Stefania, Nachbaur Magdalena, Neurauter Leah, Tan Tugba, Ünsal Kader, Winkelmann Valérie, Yavuz Asli

Ort des Austauschs (S. 7–8)

1 Michel de Certeau, „‚Räume' und ‚Orte'", in: ders., „Kunst des Handelns", Berlin 1988, S. 217–220, S. 217 f. *Ursprünglich veröffentlicht als „‚Espaces' et ‚lieux"* in *L'Invention du quotidien, Vol. 1: Arts de Faire*, Paris 1980.

Die Weichheit des Holzes (S. 40–50)

1 Vgl. Serlio, Sebastiano, *On architecture. Books VI and VII of 'Tutte l'opere d'architettura et prospetiva with 'Castrametation of the Romans' and 'The extraordinary book of doors'*, übers. u. hrsg. v. Vaughan Hart & Peter Hicks, New Haven; London 2001: Yale University Press, S. 349.
2 de L'Orme, Philibert, *Nouvelles inventions pour bien bastir …*, Paris: F. Morel. Später dann als Kapitel 10 und 11 im Œuvre: de L'Orme, Philibert (1567): *Le premier tome de l'architecture de Philibert de L'Orme*, Paris: F. Morel. Serlios 7. Buch, in dem die besonderen Dachkonstruktionen besprochen werden und die dasselbe Prinzip zeigen, erschien erst posthum 1575 in Frankfurt a.M.
3 Christian Müller, Die Entwicklung des Holzleimbaues unter besonderer Berücksichtigung der Erfindungen von Otto Hetzer – ein Beitrag zur Geschichte der Bautechnik, Diss. Bauhaus-Universität Weimar, Weimar 1998.
4 Mario Rinke, „The Form as an Imprint of an Idea", in: Mario Rinke, Florian Hauswirth (Hg.), *Formful Wood. Explorative Furniture*, Berlin 2019, S. 179–183.
5 Roshanak Haddadi, Mario Rinke, „Early Glulam for Temporary Large Scale Structures in Switzerland", in: James W. P. Campbell u. a. (Hg.), *Iron, Steel and Buildings. Studies in the History of Construction, Proceedings of the Seventh Conference of the Construction History Society*, Cambridge 2020, S. 477–488.
6 Christopher Wilk, *Plywood. A Material Story*, London 2017, S. 20–29.
7 Gerald Staib, Andreas Dörrhöfer, Markus Rosenthal, *Elemente und Systeme. Modulares Bauen – Entwurf, Konstruktion, Neue Technologien*, Basel 2008, S. 15–17.
8 Gilbert Townsend, *Carpentry and Joinery: A Practical Treatise on Simple Building Construction*, Chicago: American School of Correspondence, 1913.
9 Wolfgang Rug, „100 Jahre Holzbauentwicklung", in: Bund Deutscher Zimmermeister (Hg.), *100 Jahre Bund Deutscher Zimmermeister. 100 Jahre Verband, Holzbau, Holzbauforschung 1903–2003*, Karlsruhe 2003, S. 20–33.
10 Konrad Wachsmann and Walter Gropius, „Prefabricated Building", U.S. Patent 2,355,192, akzept. August 1944.
11 Mario Rinke, „Holzbau ist Vorfertigung", in: Mario Rinke, Martin Krammer (Hg.), *Architektur fertigen. Konstruktiver Holzelementbau*, Zürich 2020, S. 30–31.
12 Robert Schmidt III, Simon Austin, *Adaptable Architecture. Theory and Practice*, London / New York 2016, S. 35–38.
13 Institut Konstruktives Entwerfen der ZHAW, *Bauteile wiederverwenden. Ein Kompendium zum zirkulären Bauen*, Zürich 2021.
14 Mario Rinke, Towards Layered Permanence in the Sustainable Design of Buildings. *Technology|Architecture + Design*, 7(2), 2023, S. 145–149. https://doi.org/10.1080/24751448.2023.2245704.

Raum im Raum (S. 103–112)

Albers, J. (1928). Werklicher Formunterricht. Bauhaus Zeitschrift, S. 2–7, 4.
Bachelard, G. (1960). Die Poetik des Raumes. München, Carl Hanser Verlag, S. 82.
Behne, A. (1926). Der moderne Zweckbau. Berlin, Gebr. Mann Verlag, Vorwort, S. 9.
Frank, J. (1931). Das Haus als Weg und Platz. In: Der Baumeister, XXIX. München, Callwey Verlag. S. 316.
Pallasmaa, J. (2013). Die Augen der Haut – Architektur und die Sinne. Los Angeles, Atara Press.
Semper, G. (1860). Der Stil in den technischen und tektonischen Künsten. Frankfurt, Verlag für Kunst und Wissenschaft.
Van der Lahn, D. (1989). Der Architektonische Raum – Fünfzehn Lektionen über die Disposition der menschlichen Behausung. Amsterdam, Architectura & Natura.

Place of Exchange (pp. 9–10)

1 Michel de Certeau, '"Spaces" and "places"', in *The Practice of Everyday Life*, Berkeley: University of California Press, 1984, pp. 117–118, here p. 117. Originally published as '"Espaces" et "lieux"' in *L'Invention du quotidien, Vol. 1: Arts de Faire*, Paris 1980.

The Softness of Wood (pp. 41–49)

1 See *Sebastiano Serlio on Architecture, Volume Two: Books VI and VII of 'Tutte l'opere d'architettura et prospetiva'* with '*Castrametation of the Romans' and 'The Extraordinary Book of Doors'*, trans. and ed. Vaughan Hart and Peter Hicks, New Haven, CT: Yale University Press, 2001, p. 349.
2 de L'Orme, Philibert, *Nouvelles inventions pour bien bastir et à petits fraiz*, Paris: Federic Morel, 1561. Later also published as chapters 10 and 11 in his major treatise, *Le premier tome de l'architecture de Philibert de L'Orme*, Paris: Federic Morel, 1567. Serlio's 7th book, which discusses the special roof structures and illustrates the same principle, was first published posthumously in Frankfurt am Main, 1575.
3 Christian Müller, 'Die Entwicklung des Holzleimbaues unter besonderer Berücksichtigung der Erfindungen von Otto Hetzer – ein Beitrag zur Geschichte der Bautechnik', diss., Bauhaus-Universität Weimar, Weimar 1998.
4 Mario Rinke, 'The Form as an Imprint of an Idea', in: Mario Rinke and Florian Hauswirth (eds.), *Formful Wood: Explorative Furniture*, Berlin: Jovis, 2019, pp. 179–183.
5 Roshanak Haddadi and Mario Rinke, 'Early Glulam for Temporary Large-Scale Structures in Switzerland', in: James W. P. Campbell et al. (eds.), *Iron, Steel and Buildings: Studies in the History of Construction; Proceedings of the Seventh Conference of the Construction History Society*, Cambridge: Construction History, 2020, pp. 477–488.
6 Christopher Wilk, *Plywood: A Material Story*, London: Thames & Hudson, 2017, pp. 20–29.
7 Gerald Staib, Andreas Dörrhöfer, and Markus Rosenthal, 'Timber', in: *Components and Systems: Modular Construction – Design, Structure, New Technologies*, Basel: Birkhäuser, 2008, pp. 15–17.
8 Gilbert Townsend, *Carpentry and Joinery: A Practical Treatise on Simple Building Construction*, Chicago: American School of Correspondence, 1913.
9 Wolfgang Rug, '100 Jahre Holzbauentwicklung', in: Bund Deutscher Zimmermeister (ed.), *100 Jahre Bund Deutscher Zimmermeister: 100 Jahre Verband, Holzbau, Holzbauforschung 1903–2003*, Karlsruhe: Bruderverlag, 2003, pp. 20–33.
10 Konrad Wachsmann and Walter Gropius, 'Prefabricated Building', US patent no. 2,355,192, accepted August 1944.
11 Mario Rinke, 'Holzbau ist Vorfertigung', in Mario Rinke and Martin Krammer (eds.), *Architektur fertigen: Konstruktiver Holzelementbau*, Zurich: Triest Verlag, 2020, pp. 30–31.
12 Robert Schmidt III and Simon Austin, *Adaptable Architecture: Theory and Practice*, London: Routledge, 2016, pp. 35–38.
13 Institute of Constructive Design at ZHAW (ed.), *Reuse in Construction: A Compendium of Circular Architecture*, Zurich: Park Books, 2021.
14 Mario Rinke, 'Towards Layered Permanence in the Sustainable Design of Buildings', *Technology | Architecture + Design* 7, no. 2 (Fall 2023): pp. 145–149, https://doi.org/10.1080/24751448.2023.2245704.

Space Within Space (pp. 105–113)

Albers, J. (1928). 'Teaching Form through Practice'. Translated by Frederick Amrine, Frederick Horowitz and Nathan Horowitz, 2005. https://albersfoundation.org/alberses/teaching/josef-albers/teaching-form-through-practice-werklicher-formunterricht. Originally published as 'Werklicher Formunterricht'. *Bauhaus Zeitschrift für Gestaltung* 2, no. 2/3, pp. 2–7.
Bachelard, G. (1958). *The Poetics of Space*. Translated by Maria Jolas. Boston: Beacon Press, 1964. Originally published as *La Poétique de l'Espace*.
Behne, A. (1926). *The Modern Functional Building*, Translated by Michael Robinson, Santa Monica, CA: Getty Research Institute, 1996. Originally published as *Der moderne Zweckbau*.
Frank, J. (1931). 'The House as Path and Place'. Translated by Christopher Long. In *The New Space*. New Haven: Yale University Press, 2016. Originally published as 'Das Haus als Weg und Platz'. *Der Baumeister* 29 (August 1931), pp. 316–323.
Laan, Hans van der (1977). *Architectonic Space: Fifteen Lessons on the Disposition of the Human Habitat*. Translated by Richard Padovan. Leiden: E. J. Brill, 1983. Originally published as *De architectonische ruimte*.
Pallasmaa, J. (1996). *The Eyes of the Skin: Architecture and the Senses*. Chichester: Academy.
Semper, G. (1860). *Style in the Technical and Tectonic Arts; or, Practical Aesthetics*. Translated by Harry Francis Mallgrave and Michael Robinson. Los Angeles: Getty Research Institute, 2004. Originally published as *Der Stil in den technischen und tektonischen Künsten; oder, Praktische Ästhetik*.

Herausgeber Editors
Carmen Rist-Stadelmann, Urs Meister

Textbeiträge Contributions
Michael Heinzle, Livia Herle, Urs Meister, Mario Rinke,
Carmen Rist-Stadelmann, Wolfgang Schwarzmann, Machiel Spaan,
Marcella Wenger, Klaus Zwerger

Übersetzung Translation
David Koralek

Korrektorat Englisch Proofreading English
David Koralek / ArchiTrans

Korrektorat Deutsch Proofreading German
Sabine Bockmühl

Grafik Design
SJG / Joost Grootens, Dimitri Jeannottat, Julie da Silva Lenoir

Druck und Bindung Printing and binding
Wilco Art Books
Gedruckt in den Niederlanden / Printed in the Netherlands

© 2025 die Autoren / the authors und / and Park Books AG, Zürich

Produktsicherheit Product safety
Verantwortliche Person gemäss EU-Verordnung / Responsible person pursuant to EU Regulation 2023/988 (GPSR):
GVA Gemeinsame Verlagsauslieferung Göttingen GmbH & Co. KG
Postfach / Post Box 2021
37010 Göttingen
Deutschland / Germany
T +49 551 384 200 0
E info@gva-verlage.de

Park Books
Niederdorfstrasse 54
8001 Zürich
Schweiz / Switzerland
www.park-books.com

ISBN 978-3-03860-414-3

Bildnachweis Picure credits
© Stephanie Buechel (155, 156–157, 158–159, 160)
© Fabio Schober (1, 88, 89, 90, 114–115, 116, 117, 118)
© Darko Todorovic (Umschlag / Cover, 7, 8, 9, 10, 30, 31, 32, 33, 51, 52, 53, 54, 55, 68, 130, 131, 132–133, 134, 145, 146–147, 149, 151, 152–153)
Alle anderen Bilder, Pläne und Skizzen wurden von Studierenden und Dozierenden erstellt.
All other pictures, drawings and sketches by the students and authors.

Spezieller Dank an Special thanks to
Universität Liechtenstein, Vaduz
Frommelt Zimmerei und Ing. Holzbau AG, Schaan
Schreinerei Teuscher AG, Trübbach

Park Books wird vom Bundesamt für Kultur mit einem Strukturbeitrag für die Jahre 2021–2025 unterstützt.
Park Books is being supported by the Federal Office of Culture with a general subsidy for the years 2021–2025.

Alle Rechte vorbehalten; kein Teil dieser Publikation darf ohne vorherige schriftliche Zustimmung des Herausgebers in irgendeiner Form oder mit irgendwelchen Mitteln — elektronisch, mechanisch, durch Fotokopie, Aufzeichnung oder auf andere Weise — vervielfältigt, in gespeichert oder übertragen werden.
All rights reserved; no part of this publication may be reproduced, stored in a retrieval system or transmitted in any form or by any means — electronic, mechanical, photocopying, recording or otherwise — without the prior written consent of the publisher.